Not-So-Stupid
Parents

Why Your Kids Think You're Weird
and How to Prove Otherwise

Hayley DiMarco

Revell
Grand Rapids, Michigan

© 2007 by Hungry Planet

Published by Fleming H. Revell
a division of Baker Publishing Group
P.O. Box 6287, Grand Rapids, MI 49516-6287
www.revellbooks.com

Printed in the United States of America

Library of Congress Cataloging-in-Publication Data is on file at the Library of Congress, Washington, DC.

ISBN 978-0-8007-3152-6
ISBN 10: 0-8007-3152-2

Unless otherwise indicated, Scripture is taken from the *Holy Bible*, New Living Translation, copyright © 1996. Used by permission of Tyndale House Publishers, Inc., Wheaton, Illinois 60189. All rights reserved.

Scripture marked NASB is taken from the New American Standard Bible®, Copyright © 1960, 1962, 1963, 1968, 1971, 1972, 1973, 1975, 1977, 1995 by The Lockman Foundation. Used by permission.

Published in association with Yates & Yates, LLP, Literary Agents, Orange, California.

Portions of this book have been adapted from *Stupid Parents* (Revell, 2006).

Contents

Introduction: Meet My Stupid Parents   9

Part 1 The Perfect Parents: Fact or Fiction? *Before you had kids, you dreamed of being the perfect parent and giving them everything you never had. But now that they're teenagers, you are suddenly "doing it all wrong," or so it seems. Does the perfect parent exist? And is there any hope for you and your teenager?*   13

Part 2 The Art of the Deal—*You might think it's impossible, but there is a way you both can win. The art of the deal can change the way your household works.*   21

Who's the Boss?   23
Can Everyone Win?   26
Nagging Fatigue?   31
Mr. and Mrs. Embarrassing   44
The Overprotective Parent   56
Why All the Yelling?   72
Emotion Overload   77

Part 3 The Big Talk—*Wouldn't you love it if your teen would come to you with all their big questions in life? Many teens get their value system from people other than their parents because they just don't talk with them. But you can help change that.*   87

The Trust Bank   90
Give Them Attention   91
Small Talk   93

The Big Talk   95
Create Win-Win Situations   100
The Value of Memories   102
Teaching Trust   103
The Art of Negotiation   105

Part 4 Broken Trust—*If your teen has broken your trust, you can rebuild it. But it requires work from both of you.*   109

Part 5 Really Stupid Parents—*No one is perfect, and sometimes as a parent you can really mess up. When you do something to your life that affects the life of your teen, how can you help them cope?*   115

The Hurt of Divorce   117
The Harm of Drugs and Alcohol   128
The Danger of Being Overworked   129

Part 6 Single Parents—*Being a single parent can be a real challenge for you, but what does your teen think about the situation? Learn some candid truths about being the only parent at home.*   137

Living with a Single Parent   138
Parents Who Are Looking for Love   143
Stepparents and Your Teen   147

The End—*or as some call it, the conclusion. But it's really just the beginning for your relationship with your teen.*   155

Honor your father and mother. Then you will live a long, full life.

—the fifth commandment (Exodus 20:12)

IntroDuction

Meet My Stupid Parents

Slamming doors, pouting faces, and emotional roller coasters—every parent of a teenager knows exactly what it's like to be considered stupid at some point or another. Sometimes you might even *feel* stupid when it comes to your kid's life. Sure, you were a teenager once, but my, how times have changed. The things (iPods, Xboxes, cell phones, etc.) and situations that your kids are growing up with are radically different from the things and situations you encountered when you were their age. So **how do you see eye to eye with someone who seems so completely disenchanted with your knowledge and foresight?** Some parents just disengage, opting to leave the kid alone until things cool down, while others tighten up the reigns and attempt to garner more control of their loose-cannon teenager.

Now, before we go any further, I don't claim to be an expert on raising teenagers. I've never done it myself (though my daughter will ultimately reach her teen years, God willing). But what I do claim to know is what your teenager is thinking and some of the reasons why they do what they do—or in some cases don't do what they need to do. Where does this knowledge come from, you ask? Well, I was trained to connect with the teen mind at a little shoe company called Nike, I created a multimillion-dollar teen book brand at a major book publisher, and my company Hungry Planet has sold over a half a million books in our first three years, mainly to a generation of young adults that is accused of being disinterested in reading. I share this not out of pride but rather out of respect for you, the parent of a teen, to make sure you know that this won't be a waste of your time. The observations and advice that went into *Stupid Parents* and the book you're reading now come from speaking and listening to thousands of teens in person and through my websites like www.askhayley.com. What *Not-So-Stupid Parents* will attempt to do is to teach you what your child is thinking and how to better communicate your love to them, even if your teen doesn't want to hear it.

In *Stupid Parents: Why They Just Don't Understand and How You Can Help*, I introduced teenagers to the concept of learning to thrive while living under authority. I walked kids through sample conversations, opportunities, and disagreements in order to help them better relate to you and thrive with you. If you bought that book for your teen before buying this one, I hope you saw a significant change in their attitude. In the same vein, *Not-So-Stupid Parents* will help you better understand what your teen is now thinking and understanding about their relationship to someone in authority over them. By reading *Not-So-Stupid Parents* after or in conjunction with your teen reading the youth version of the book, you will also be able to have more meaningful conversations with them about the topics discussed in their book. And at the end of the chapters in this book are conversation starters and ideas to consider that you can use to work through the chapters with your child. Even if they've already read their version, the questions will allow you to start meaningful conversations and hopefully open doors of understanding where before there were deadbolts.

If your child hasn't read *Stupid Parents* or you think they will balk at it, then may I suggest that you don't hand them the book and tell them to read it. A defiant child will most often do the opposite of what they are told, especially when it comes to reading what they might consider to be parental propaganda. In order to avoid that stigma, I suggest not handing them the book but leaving it out somewhere for them to "stumble upon." When you catch them picking it up, you might even say something like, "Oh, I don't think I want you reading something like that. I don't like the word *stupid*. And I certainly don't look like that parent on the cover!" I know, reverse psychology seems shameful, but it works, trust me.

In *Stupid Parents* your teenager will read about the fact that your so-called stupidity isn't stupidity; it's just a misunderstanding of goals and roles. What I teach them, I would wager, is exactly what you've been telling them for years, but for some reason when they hear it from me, it sounds different. Consider me your sister who visits for the holidays from the big city; what she says just seems more relevant, even when it's the same thing you're saying. I'll go into the reasons why that is more as we move through the book.

In the meantime, I hope you forgive my flagrant use of the word *stupid* to describe you and instead find hope and peace in the pages of this book.

Meet My Stupid Mom

My mom can drive me crazy. I mean, how hard is it to download an attachment off of email? Believe me, very hard, if you're my mother. Don't get me wrong; my mom is great. She's so kind and caring. She always took such good care of me. She loves me. She fed me and clothed me and acted as both mom and dad to me. She's a jewel. But sometimes she can drive me nuts. And I have to confess that I haven't always been the nicest person in return. I lose my patience with her. I've yelled. I've huffed and I've puffed. Everything short of blowing the house down. And I know she hates it. It has put a strain on our relationship. So I'm writing from experience when it comes to stupid parents. Today I would never call my mom stupid (except in the heading of this section!), even if she can't figure out how to reboot or defrag her computer, but when I was in high school I wanted to. Truth is, she is very bright; she's just not part of my generation, so a lot of new things stump her. I mean, she didn't grow up with computers in the classroom. More like pencils and slide rules. Ah, the simpler times. But it's no wonder she doesn't get the things that come so easily to my generation.

It seems like the parent-child relationship can be the most exasperating of all relationships, probably because we're so close to each other and in each other's faces for so many hours a day. If you're like me and you want some peace at home, then have hope. It can be done—it just might take a little work and a little understanding. So stick with me and we'll see if we just can't put the "not-so" in front of one more "stupid parent"!

The Perfect Parents

Fact or Fiction?

PART 1

The Other S Word

stupid: a bad word used to describe someone you don't currently like, who is frustrating you, or who just doesn't understand

It's not the bad word that adults sometimes make it out to be; really, to a teen it just means you don't get it. But that aside, I know how parents hate this word, especially when it describes them, so know that I urge your teen to avoid it at all costs. You're not stupid; they're just emotional! And this too shall pass.

Remember the days before you had children? The days when you dreamed of one day bringing home that perfect little bundle of joy? You dreamt of those beautiful little fingers, those chubby toes, and that wonderful baby smell, and you told yourself, "Someday my dream will come true. I will have a child of my own, and I will give them everything I never had—materially, emotionally, and even spiritually." Preparing for a baby can be one of the most exciting times of life. But now those memories are close to a distant memory as you tackle life of a different kind: life with a teenager.

If you're reading this book, you might be at the end of your rope. You probably have issues that need attention. You still want to give your child everything you didn't get. **You want them to grow up strong, healthy, and successful, but the battle is of a different kind, and you just don't know where to turn.** It seems like everything you do now is wrong. Your child might not have said it to your face, but maybe they've uttered it under their breath—"You are so stupid! You just don't get it!" And it's the worst feeling in the world. But I've got your back. You're not so stupid as they think. What we have here is a failure to communicate. You are a good parent; after all, you've picked up

this book in order to work on things, and that's a sign of a good parent. Stupid parents don't go the extra mile. They don't seek to better understand their children. But you, my friend, are a truly good parent. Congratulations!

I believe that because of your desire to better understand your child, things will get better. The family that wants to change can have tremendous hope. So take heart—the parent that you want to be might not be too far off. Cut yourself some slack. Take a deep breath, and utter a prayer of hope and thanksgiving. You can become not-so-stupid to your teenager.

Remember, my qualifications for helping you with your teenager aren't rooted in a thriving family counseling practice or successfully shipping off six teens to college and healthy careers as doctors, teachers, and lawyers. I'm not a parenting expert, and this is not a book on how to parent your child. Surprised? Just wait. It isn't a book on parenting, but it *is* a book on *understanding* your teenager, which I hope will help you parent better. Rather than thinking of me as an expert on parenting, consider me your expert on teenagers. I know more about what the average teenager is thinking and feeling than the average joe. I have years of experience in talking to, researching, and writing for teens just like yours, and because of that I hope I have some insight that might just help you out.

Before we get started, let me just tell you that no matter what they say, your teenagers don't hate you. They *love* you. They don't want "nothing to do with you"; they want you in their lives. They just don't know how to show it or, as funny as this sounds, say it. Sure, they might feel angry, hurt, and bitter about some things, but at the bottom of it all, they are still your baby. They still need you and want you. And no matter what, you haven't gone so wrong that a little course adjustment can't help. Teens don't always have the best skills when it comes to communication. Their feelings and their hormones are bouncing around inside of them like a ping-pong ball in a tornado, and they don't always know how to explain them or live with them. And **because you are so safe and so close, they tend to take out their emotional and hormonal frustrations on you.** And honestly, don't we all tend to do the same thing to those we love? They know that no matter how badly they behave or disengage, you will always have to love them, and that is a safe, wonderful place to be.

So take heart—deep down they really do need and want you, no matter how they are expressing it right now. And the truth of the matter is that this too shall pass. Your teen won't stay a teen any longer than they stayed

Damaged Kids

This book was written for the average parent of the average teenager. I am well aware that some teens need more serious help than others. If you have a teen who is violent, suicidal, or emotionally unstable, this book won't solve your problems. Please seek the counsel of trained professionals who understand the kinds of problems your teenager faces. *Not-So-Stupid Parents* is really for the parents who face the average, run-of-the-mill bickering, nagging, and difficulty with normal, run-of-the-mill teenagers.

a baby. Soon they will be out on their own, and you will slowly become more a trusted confidant and companion than a stupid parent.

In some parts of this book you might feel like I'm siding with your teenager, but I'm not—I'm siding with the family. **In the book *Stupid Parents: Why They Just Don't Understand and How You Can Help*, I talk to teens about learning to live and love under authority** (that's you!). I share with them many insights on how to better respect and respond to you in order to help create a peaceful home. I ask a lot of them in *Stupid Parents*, all with the goal of helping them to get what they want, and that's a better relationship with you and a safe, comfortable place to call home. As I considered all that I was telling them in that book, I thought about how much more effective their actions would be if their parents were in on it. I imagined some parents seeing a change in their child and out of habit thinking, *What's up with him? Is he trying to get something out of me?* I imagined that a drastic change in how they communicate with you might seem impossible and therefore somehow manipulative. I also understood that without the parent participating in changing the relationship, success was much less likely. And so I decided to write this companion book to help parents and teens get on the same page. Here you will find both excerpts of the teen book and insights on what your actions and words do to the mind and heart of your teenager.

My goal, and I hope yours as well, is for you to learn to meet your child in the middle—not always, but more often—so that there can be some growth on both sides. Some of my insights might seem ridiculous, but I urge you to give these ideas a try, because if you keep doing what you're doing, you'll keep getting what you're getting. And my hunch is that it isn't good enough. So please take my words as a potential lifeline to your teenager's heart and do with them what you will. When you feel like I'm siding with your teen, know that when reading their book, they feel like I'm siding with you. That's because both books are all about helping each of you to walk a day in each other's shoes, as the saying goes. I believe that the parent is ultimately the final authority and the teen's responsibility is obedience and respect. But I also believe that as parents we should raise a child in the way they should go—that is, understand them inside and out so we can treat each one in a way that fits his or her own unique personality and temperament. And one of the best ways to do that is to understand how the mind of a teenager works. So with that said,

I hope you enjoy your time here and that your family life blossoms as you experiment with some of these concepts.

You will notice that **at the end of the chapters are some final ideas to consider, sometimes including discussion questions or topics.** Your teen's book doesn't have these. They are for you to use as fodder for conversations and discovery. These questions are best used in a casual situation. Don't make a big deal out of these conversations; make them natural. Everyday conversations make a greater impact in a teenager's mind and don't freak them out like a planned "talk" can do. So just bring up these discussion topics throughout your day-to-day life. If you have a child who loves planned talks and wants to work on the books together, then by all means, go for it. You know your kid best. All I can tell you is that most teenagers fear "the talk," whatever the subject, but love when you take interest in their day-to-day lives. If they shut you down when you ask this stuff, don't shut down yourself. They might just not be in the mood. Save the discussion for later. Remember, you're the adult here; you're the one who has the emotional and mental control of yourself. *You're the mature one—otherwise your teen would be called an adult!* So don't get upset or hurt if they aren't in the mood for talking. And please, please, don't ever give up! One day they will appreciate your talks.

So enjoy, and let's prove to your kids that you're one of the *Not-So-Stupid Parents!*

Ideas to Consider

Your grandkids—Talk to your kids about their future family. How will they raise their kids? If you have a daughter, ask her if she will work outside the home if she has children. Why or why not? Will they let their kids do this or that? Essentially put them in your position without saying that directly. Just have a casual conversation about their hopes and dreams. It will give you insight into their needs and desires as a kid. Remember, you once had ideas about how you would raise your kids based on what you did or didn't like about how your parents did it. So talk to your kids about their ideas.

This kind of conversation works best with girls, because they are often already fantasizing about marriage and family and will probably be able to tell you instantly what they will do with their family. Boys might be clueless. They aren't always thinking about the future, and certainly not about their future kids, but you can give it a shot and see what comes of the conversation. Try talking about your memories of wanting a car and wanting more freedom as a teen, how you were sure you were going to be different when you had kids, and so on.

Other parents—Talk to your kids about their friends' parents. What do they like about how those parents interact with their kids? What do they dislike? These kinds of questions can flow naturally out of situations involving other kids and their parents. Their answers should give you insight into what they are missing or wanting from you. But the conversation also gives you a chance to explain why you've chosen not to be the way other sets of parents are. This is a chance not only for them to teach you what they need but also for you to teach them who you are and why you do what you do. Remember, conversation builds relationship. Be there for your teens, and they will respect you more and more.

The Art
of the Deal

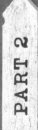

Who's the Boss?

Everyone must learn to live under authority, unless they go the way of the Unabomber. In order to graduate from school or hold a job, your child must learn to live under authority. And **their first and most formative experience with authority is with you.** If they can learn to function with you happily and peacefully, then they'll be more successful in the future. The way you interact with them and they with you will affect how much money they make, what kind of jobs they get and keep, and how comfortable they are at home.

In *Stupid Parents* I talked to your teenager about two common but stupid ways that young people react to authority: (1) by quitting and (2) by overpowering. Take a look at this excerpt to see what I told them.

> ### Quitters Never Win
>
> When it comes to a job, you can always quit if you don't like your boss. I used to know a girl who would quit every time her boss did or said something she didn't like. And each time she would have to hit the pavement and find another job, starting all over at the bottom of the pay scale. Because of her constant discontent with people in authority over her, she never stayed anywhere long enough to move up. She never made more money or got a better position. She always stayed at the bottom of the ladder and just jumped from one ladder to another.
>
> Now, it was her option to jump ship when the orders from the captain got to be too much for her to handle, and that's the beauty of a job. You can move to another one anytime you like. But when it comes to your parents, you

don't have that luxury. **You can't tell them you quit and move to the house next door every time they tick you off.** You're stuck with the ones you've got. The parents you've got are the parents you'll always have.

What your kids need to understand is that **unless they have a huge trust fund independent of their parents' control, it's probably best to figure out how to get along rather than bailing out and trying to do it all on their own or spending all their free time arguing with you over stupid stuff.**

They also need to understand your authority. Here's what I told them about that:

Overpowering Your Parents?

Another stupid way some people try to handle someone in authority over them is to try to overpower them, to take over the relationship, to wrangle the power away from them. Let's just make it crystal clear right now: Any attempt to overcome the power of those in authority over you—parents, teachers, bosses, police, etc.—is a giant waste of your time. Think of it like this. When you go to McDonald's in the middle of the afternoon and want the Big Breakfast, you can't overcome the fact that they won't give it to you. You don't have the power to change the hours they serve breakfast. And believe me, any attempt to do so is futile. They just look at you with a blank look and say, "Sorry, no hotcakes for you!" It can't be done. The same goes for your job. You can't set corporate policy or the hours you work. And many a fool has tried to overcome the power of the police only to end up facedown on the ground looking at his reflection in those shiny black boots. Face it, if you try to overpower the authority in your life, you lose.

As a parent, you are charged with teaching this to your child. Like it or not, you control things, and any attempt to take that power from you can and should only make things worse. They don't pay the bills, you do—hence you're the boss. So understanding your position of power is crucial. Only when you know your position can you start to make the relationship better. Your child has to understand that they have to stop thinking that in order to be happy, they have to overcome your power and control. That would only be a temporary fix; eventually the world would teach them something different. Living under authority has to be learned sooner or later. So you are doing your child a favor by helping them learn the skill of managing themselves when someone else is in charge of them. The sooner they (the child) can give up control to those entrusted with them (you), the sooner they can thrive in a world built on that system. You are their training ground. So don't let them bully you into feeling bad that you are the boss. Until they move out, that is the way it has to be.

In a family where those roles are allowed to be reversed, we see only chaos and disaster. Young people who are allowed to usurp the authority of their parents can become a menace to the family and to society. If your teen has control of you, that has to stop today. You aren't doing them any favors by letting them have it their way against your better judgment. You are only delaying the inevitable, and the fight they try to pick with the world will be much more dangerous than the fight they pick with you. Whether your teen knows it or not, they have a deep need for a foundation of discipline and control from you, or they will spin out of control. So let's walk through how to take charge and be an authority that your child can live under peacefully.

Can Everyone Win?

There are ways that you both can win. Your home doesn't have to be a tyranny. You can create win-win situations where both of you feel like you are meeting in the middle. I call it *the art of the deal*, and the object is to make an agreement where everyone feels like they are getting what they want out of the situation (or at least something they can live with). Think back to a game of checkers or one-on-one basketball with your child when he or she was little. Even though you saw moves on the checkerboard that would hand you the win every time or you could back your daughter down in the paint and dunk on her as her true Shaq Daddy, truth be told, if you keep winning all the time, the person you are playing with won't want to play anymore. They might even hate the game (parenting and the family unit) for life. Losing isn't fun, and doing it over and over again is the worst.

Many teens are sick and tired of losing. They might feel like they never get their way. Or maybe you feel like that. If there is friction in the relationship, then how can anyone really feel like they're winning, even if they do ultimately get what they want? We all have something to gain from getting away from the friction. If you can go home at the end of a long day and not have to yell or argue with your kid, then you'll feel like you've won, and so will they. What you want is for them to do the right thing, and what they want is as little trauma as possible—but then I bet so do you. I mean, you're tired, you're overworked, and the last thing you want is another argument. So let's see if we can stop the screaming.

In *Stupid Parents* I taught your kids that understanding what you have or can offer another person is called leverage. And they can use it with you just like in a business deal. Finding out what you really want is crucial, because without giving you what you want or at least trying to work toward it, the battles will continue to rage. **I'm not trying to teach them manipulation but an understanding of conflict management and thriving under authority.** It's important for your child to understand exactly what you want from them so that they can give it to you. If I can help them to understand that giving you what you desire helps them to get what *they* want—which is peace, trust, and growing freedom—then maybe we can help the entire family thrive.

So **don't be shocked when your child starts to comply with you.** They aren't playing some kind of trick; they are testing to see whether if they *do* give you what you want, you will give them what *they* want, at least to some degree. My hope is that as they start to see that you are not unreasonable but logical, they will start to learn how best to interact with you.

I find that the best way to teach a teenager is not by ultimatums and drawing the line but by education. They are at an age of understanding. They are reading Dostoyevsky and *War and Peace* in class; surely they are fairly intelligent beings by now. And though by no means do I consider them adults, I do consider them adults in training, which means they need some exercises. They need some options to learn by, places to fall down and get back up again. It was hard to let them fall down when they were toddlers, and now it will be just as hard to let them try their strength at making adult decisions. That said, I believe that for the mind of the teenager, **the best tactic for getting them to do something is to show them the facts and the results of choices.** In all my books I like to fill them in on what's going on in the minds of those around them, including God, and help them to make decisions for themselves based on those facts. I find that a teen who makes up their own mind (with an adult's guidance, of course) is more likely to stick to those decisions than one who is told what to do.

So let's dive into an analysis of the family dynamic. Actions and reactions. Cause and effect.

As adults we know that our actions greatly affect what happens to us. The trouble is that teens sometimes feel powerless, as if life just comes at them and they have nothing to do with what happens, although that isn't always the case. How we react and interact with people and situations greatly affects what happens to us as a result. This isn't a concept we are born understanding, and many teens never learn it. I once worked with a sixteen-year-old girl who had just gotten out of juvenile detention for hitting another girl with a baton. She had a hard time at home, fought with her mom constantly, and didn't know how to control her anger. I was surprised how shocked she was after doing a little exercise.

I had her write down all her actions in the past month in one column and the results of those actions in a column next to them. Then I had her write down what outcomes she would prefer to have in her life. After that I asked her to look at her list. If doing what she was doing was giving her what she was getting, did she think that if she kept doing those kinds of things, the outcomes would magically change? She looked at me in complete and utter disbelief. "No," she said, and then she smiled. "I never looked at it that way. If I keep doing these things on the left, I'll keep getting these things on the right. Wow! I don't want to do those things anymore."

No one had ever pointed out to her the effect of the things she herself was doing. After that we worked on new ways of reacting to people in order for her to get what she wanted. In a matter of days, her life was on the mend. Even her relationship with her mother. I believe that if only I could have had the ear of the mother as well, that family could have been healed forever. But I've found that without the full participation of the parent on the same wavelength, it's almost impossible to change things permanently. Parents who aren't set on the same goal as the child just pull the willing child back into the same dysfunctional mess all over again. That's why I'm so glad you've picked up this book. Your participation in implementing the ideas your child is reading in *Stupid Parents* will double your chances at reversing the trends of anger and frustration in your home.

Below is the table I encourage kids and parents to fill out in order to better understand that what they're currently doing isn't working. I'm not assuming for this exercise that either one of you is the perfect communicator, so don't feel like I'm picking on you here. In *Stupid Parents* I ask your child to do the same analysis of their reactions to you. **Conflict management requires taking an honest look at how we react to people who disagree with us.** So I encourage you to do that as we work through this book. Here's what I want you to do. Write down some of the ways your kids react to your actions, like this:

YOUR ACTION	THEIR RESPONSE
Screaming as they walk up the stairs	A slammed door and an angry child
Continually nagging them to get things done	An apparently lazy child who won't take any initiative

As you start to work through the book and these things come up, it might be a good exercise to fill this out with your child. Helping them to see cause and effect can really help them to make better decisions. For an easier, less confrontational exercise, I'd suggest doing this with a situation in their life that doesn't involve you—maybe involving someone at school or a friend. That way you become more of a life coach and less of a nagging parent in their eyes. And really, isn't that what a parent really is, a life coach? The more you can work with your child to learn how to manage relationships other than your own, the better your relationship with them will be. Remember, even though they might not show it, they really do look to you for guidance and wisdom. If you are teaching them *how* to do things themselves instead of always telling them *what* to do, they will be much more receptive to your advice.

When it comes to the art of the deal, it's also important to realize what kind of commodity you are dealing with—that is, what you have that *they* want and vice versa. Let's have a look at a few scenarios and see if we can't start to better understand why you do some of the things you do when it comes to your kids and why they behave the way they do. Remember that the object of these principles is to get you and your teenager to stop fighting and start communicating.

Nagging Fatigue?

Nagging—how's that working for you? Seems like the more you ask them to do things, the less they do, right? Could it be that you have the laziest teenager on the block? Or are they just trying to be difficult? Chances are, neither is true, at least at first. As your child hits puberty, a lot of things start happening in their bodies and minds. In addition to all the changes that I'm sure you are well aware of are also the added pressures of school and planning for the future. Life suddenly isn't all about Play-Doh and playdates; it starts to take on an air of seriousness and impending doom (aka responsibility). Of course, their minds are still young and not fully developed, so in part they are still kids—kids on the cusp of becoming big people.

What a lot of parents don't understand (or at least don't recall) about being a teenager is that it can be very exhausting. Your body and mind are growing at such a rate that you are physically and mentally taxed. Add to that the desire for social activity as well as the responsibility of school, and you have one tired puppy. Many teens, not just yours, can be found sound asleep on a Saturday afternoon, unable to pull themselves out from under the covers till 2:00 or 3:00 p.m. I remember the days. I wasn't a bad kid. I got good grades, got along well with my parents (when they weren't divorcing), and didn't covet breaking the rules, but boy did I covet my sleep. I felt like I could sleep forever, so tired was my mind and body. Do you remember the days?

The thing I encourage parents to remember is that **though your teens don't by any means have the responsibilities that you have, they might just feel the same kind of exhausting pressure that you feel without possessing the maturity and perspective to deal with it.** So keep that in mind as you begin to decide what responsibilities and family requirements you want

to bestow on them. Chores and duties in the home are a great way to teach your teenager responsibility and life skills, but if you aren't aware of your child's physical makeup at this time of life, you might find that getting them to do things around the house seems like a losing battle.

So what's the art of the deal have to say about this situation? Am I saying that parents should just lay off and allow their kids to do whatever they want? No. Most certainly not. Actually, what I tell your kids is that they need to respect you and stop avoiding the work. I want your kids to obey you and to understand that that obedience is a training

Teen Talk

I'm not as lazy as you think. I really do have a lot on my plate, and I just wish you understood and respected the things in my life enough to give me a break on the things in your life you want me to handle. I'm not trying to avoid you or disobey you; I'm just trying to manage the responsibilities and things in my life that make me who I am.

—Your Child

ground for their future. As I said before, living well under authority is an art form that will make your life much more successful.

Below is a list of things I have given your teenager to consider when it comes to the nagging problems in the family. This is directly from the teen book *Stupid Parents*. I want you to read this so you understand what I am telling them. Essentially, this is what you need to help them understand. So have a look at what they are reading, and then I'll follow that up with some notes just for you.

> **1.** Nagging happens because your parents feel like they have to ask you over and over again to do something. They have to ask you over and over again because you didn't do anything the *first* time they asked you.

Mr. Obvious Says—"So do it the first time they ask you!"

Sure, that makes the most sense. Do it the first time. If you can make a point of doing what they ask right when they ask you, then you can avoid tons of nagging. I mean, what can they nag you about if you did what they asked? Trouble is, you don't always feel like you have time to do it right when they ask. You have a life, other things that have to get done, so you can't always do it *right that second*. And parents don't always understand that. So the next day they ask again, thinking you must have forgotten or you would have done it. And if you don't do it this time, they really blow their top because they've asked you twice and still you didn't do anything. In their minds they are thinking, *How hard is it to do what I've asked?* Their reasoning goes something like this. "When I'm at work and I get asked to do something by my boss, I'd darn well better do it or I'll lose my job." It's just the way their minds work—when asked by someone in authority over you to do something, you do it.

They might work overtime, go in early, or complain about their workload continually because *they*, just like you, are being told what to do by someone who has power over them. Only for them, if they don't do it, it could mean getting fired, whereas for you, there's no chance of that. But that's part of their frustration. They understand that if you can't learn *now* how to do things when you're asked, then how will you ever hold down a job where you're being asked to do stuff all day long? How will you support yourself when you're ready to go out on your own? See, their nagging isn't all about bossing you around. It's one part needing your help to get things done and one part wanting to teach you some skills so you can get and keep that killer job that you're going to want in order to get out on your own.

You might be playing your itty-bitty violin between your fingers right now saying, "Would you like more cheese with your whine?" But whether you care about their trials and worries or not, you need to trust me on this: Knowing where they are coming from and what they are feeling will help you in the art of the deal. Remember, it's all about figuring out what they want or need in order to better get what you want or need. It's like the market economy you learned about in Social Studies. If you have what someone else wants or can supply some kind of service that they need, then you can sell them that good or service in order to get what you want or need in return. In the family environment the exchange of goods and services is not just for money but for something sometimes far more valuable—peace and quiet. You want it, and they'll give it to you if you give them what they want. Win-win!

Makes sense, right? As your child grows up, she will have more and more required of her, as we all do. And over time she'll learn that if you don't do things when asked, you are more likely to forget to do them. That's why we have day planners, PDAs, and schedules. As adults we keep track of all our responsibilities, meetings, and projects so we don't have to be nagged by our bosses. Teaching your child how to best manage their time is a great gift for a parent to give. You might want to help them by giving them a day planner or a PDA or by posting a sheet with responsibilities on the wall. But I urge you to also consider the makeup of your child. You know them better than I do. If they are a good kid who works hard at school and work and growing up, consider not piling on more to "keep them busy." Remember that these school years are usually looked back on as "glory days," the best of your life—that is, they are the most free for most of us. They are a time when we can learn, grow, socialize, and have fun. We explore who we are and what we want to be. And being burdened with more work at home can deprive your child of the freedom that comes with just being a kid. So **when you start to assign tasks or chores for your kids, think about what will help them grow as an individual and what will allow them to still enjoy being a kid** before all the cares of the world get added to their plates. This is an individual choice and will vary based on size of family and necessity. The thing to remember about your kids is that they need and crave boundaries and discipline but also tender love and understanding. If you truly want to raise a child in the way they should go, then you will take into consideration their temperament and their stage of life and act accordingly.

The ultimate goal of this book is to bring peace to the home and help you to better relate to your child so that you can enjoy one another's presence while you have it. If you have a relationship that is sorely bruised or damaged, you might want to consider changing the way you are doing things. As I always say, if you keep doing what you're doing, you'll keep getting what you're getting. Has that been good enough?

Here's a little taste of what I told teens about nagging:

> **2. Ignoring them just makes it worse.** They sound like a broken record. You've heard it before, so you shut them off. Just ignore them. It seems to make more sense. I mean, why listen to the nagging when all it does is frustrate you? But I've got news for ya—when you ignore them, you only make it worse. It's like this. If I'm in a closed-in stairwell at school and the doors are all locked, I'm going to start knocking to see if anyone can let me out. And if I can hear them talking on the other side of the door so I know they are there but they are just ignoring me, I'm going to start yelling at them and pounding on the door. And if they still don't open it for me, I'm going to start yelling and pounding even louder. The more they ignore me, the louder I get, because I want to get out of there. Catch the visual? When you think you are being ignored or someone can't hear you, you talk or yell even louder.
>
> Same goes for the nagging. When you ignore their requests, especially if they've been repeated, then they feel like they need to keep on you because you aren't listening. It's a frustrating experience not to be listened to. I'm sure you know what I'm talking about. For me, it's probably the worst feeling in the world. You know when you're trying to tell somebody something or prove a point and they just keep saying "Yeah, yeah, whatever" and try to talk over you or act like they won't listen to you? That drives me nuts. I used to start screaming and getting in their face. It makes me feel so helpless; I just want to grab them by the shoulders

and shake them to make them listen. Sound familiar? It's awful not to be listened to.

That said, the same goes for you, Mom and Dad. Remember how awful it feels not to be listened to, and take the time to listen to your child. Know their schedule and empathize with their workload. And consider that this is the time of their life when they are exploring not only education but also relationships and interpersonal communication. It might seem like a waste of good time to spend all those hours with their friends, but it's teaching them about people. And you can teach them just as much by listening to their stories and sharing your wisdom about humanity and how to relate to others as you can by asking them to bear some of the responsibility around the house. Again, understanding your child can help you determine the best way to teach them. So take the time to get to know about their life when they are away from you, and use the things they are going through in their world to teach them about growing up.

So don't ignore them when they ask you stuff. You only make things harder on yourself. Instead, here's what I want you to do:

3. Shut up. Yep. I know it's hard. But shut up. **Listen to them.** Hear what they want from you without saying, "But Mom . . . !" When you shut up, you make things a lot easier on yourself.

Teenspeak

4. Listen to them. Okay, now that your mouth is shut, hear them out. Let them tell you what they want and why. It makes them feel better. And when they feel better, you'll feel better. It's part of the market economy. Treat your customers with respect, and they will continue to come back for more. If you want to do repeat business with your parents, then treat them well, and you'll be amazed how much more freedom you will get.

5. Look 'em in the eyes. Adults *love* this. When you look an adult in the eyes, they feel listened to. But more importantly, it makes you look more like an adult. Little kids let their eyes wander, and it makes them look immature, unable to handle responsibility and important stuff. You want them to respect you and start to treat you like an adult? Then above all else, look 'em in the eyes. All adults. Your parents, your teachers, the bank teller, the police officer. Everyone. Always look them in the eyes, and you'll go up a notch on the respect-o-meter.

6. Apologize. When you get nagged, apologize. Tell them you are sorry you didn't do it earlier. Making excuses doesn't help the situation. So when you *briefly* explain *why* you didn't do what they asked, don't whine and try to make them feel sorry for you. Remember, this is supposed to sound like an apology. I know you desperately want to prove to them that you had more important things to do, but be careful, because trying to fight for your rights only ticks them off more, and then you lose. So keep it short and just apologize for not doing it sooner, "because (fill in the blank)." No whining! You only want them to hear that you had a conflict but that you are sorry. This can stave off a potential battle before it starts.

7. Feel for them. The next step is to make them feel better by showing them you understand their frustration—that way they don't have to explain it to *you*. This avoids a lecture. When you try to understand where they are coming from and tell them you do, they no longer have anything to lecture you about. So tell them you understand how frustrating it must be to them and how you understand that they really wanted this or that thing done. If you can sympathize with people, you can get a lot further in life. It causes them to let down their guard. Especially your parents—they won't know what to think of your newfound sensitivity. It's definitely a great bargaining chip in the art of the deal. But be genuine; they don't need to know that you're bargaining. Try to understand the stress in their lives as you also remember that understanding is what you need to get what you want: peace and quiet at home.

Mr. Obvious Wraps It Up in Case You Missed It: "Just do it! Whatever they are nagging you about, just go do it. The sooner you do it, the sooner they will stop nagging. No-brainer! You want them to shut up, get up, and get it done."

This list is essential for your child to master. It will not only make life at home more peaceful but also give them a huge leg up in the world. These are the traits of a confident, intelligent human being, and your child will greatly benefit from behaving like this with all adults. If your kid isn't used to looking you or any adult in the eyes, that's where it has to start. It's a sign of respect and confidence. Don't let them get away with looking away. Some parents worry about being too hard on their kids, especially if they're hyper-moody, but the truth is, you can't let them manipulate you into not being the adult. Moody or not, they need to learn the art of communication and respect.

These skills are good for all of us, even grown-ups. So listen to your child, look them in the eyes, and try a little empathy. It will not only help the situation but also show them by example how it's done.

Top 10 Things Parents Nag About

- Chores
- Homework
- Irresponsibility
- Clothes
- Curfew
- Friends
- Hair
- Sex
- Dating
- Money

Ideas to Consider

Stress test—Having trouble getting your teenager to do things? Learn more about their schedule. Talk to them about the things they have to do. I have a feeling the more you understand their schedule, the more you'll see why they might not be doing as much as you'd like around the house. Be reasonable in your requests. Understand their stressed-out life, but also find ways to help alleviate the stress. The patterns they are learning now are the foundation for their adulthood. If you want to save them from being run ragged the rest of their lives, you might want to talk to them about scaling back a little—and not so they can do more around the house but so that they can learn to rest, learn to socialize with their family, and learn that go-go-go isn't the best that life has to offer.

For example, your teenager might feel pressure to be involved in a lot of extracurricular activities, from soccer to basketball to swimming. But what is that teaching them about life, and what is it doing to your family? You are the parent, so if you feel that they are too harried in life, you have the ability to make them cut back on things. You might find some resistance, but you might also find relief. Nagging is never effective and never any fun. So talk often to your teenager about their life, and do your best to understand them and find ways of helping them enjoy what's left of their childhood and their time at home with the family.

Stand your ground—A lot of nagging happens because parents don't mean what they say. Teens are quick to spot weak parents who say, "Do this or else," and then never follow through on the "or else." So practice standing your ground—saying what you mean and meaning what you say. If you say no TV if they don't clean up their room, and they don't clean up their room, remove the TV. You will do your teenager a great deal of good if you teach them that their actions have real consequences and not only threatened ones. They might be angry at you at first, but over time they will appreciate your consistency. You will give them a firm foundation to stand on instead of one they can't predict.

Mr. anD Mrs. EmBarrassing

It's sad but true: **most of us will embarrass our kids at some point in our lives.** We might do it on purpose because we can, or it might be out of our control. Either way, chances are that every parent at some point or another will become an embarrassment. Some relationships will be unaffected, as many teens just shrug off the goofy things you do, but others will suffer because of your teen's fear of what you'll do next, and that's what's really at issue here. It can feel terrible when they cringe because of something you said in front of their friends. And it can put a real strain on the relationship if they desperately don't want to be seen with you out of sheer embarrassment. You may or may not be aware of how your behavior negatively impacts your teenager and therefore your relationship, but if you want things to change between you, then a sober inspection of the things you do might help the problem areas of your relationship. Here is a list of things to consider. Do any of these remind you of anybody?

TOP 10 Ways Parents Embarrass Their Teenagers

- Yelling at them in public
- Dressing like a geek
- Trying to be "cool"
- Being too loud and drawing attention to yourself and them
- Being too affectionate in public
- Treating them like a little kid in front of their friends
- Grilling their girlfriend or boyfriend
- Saying something stupid in front of their friends
- Drinking too much or doing drugs
- Not taking care of your body

If any of those sound like you, then you might want to consider tweaking your habits a little. I'm not saying you have to change your personality; after all, I think a little embarrassment can do a person good. But if you don't like your child's opinion of you or you are starting to think that it would be nice *not* to embarrass them anymore, then let's talk about some ways you can do that. But before we do, let me just share with you what I told your kids in *Stupid Parents*. Notice that throughout this book I'm asking both you and your kids to give a little. I don't expect both of you to give all the time, but the more you can meet in the middle, the easier the relationship will be. So with that in mind, here is a rundown of what I told *them* about *your* embarrassing moments:

> **1. Remember that no one cares.** . . . Believe me, they aren't spending all their energy thinking about you and what your parent did. So get over it. If anything, it just gives everyone a good laugh. Growing older means becoming your own person. As you age you start to move farther and farther from your parents until eventually you literally move away. It's part of growing

up; you can't always be attached at their hip. The same goes for your feelings. You can't feel attached at the hip emotionally to your parents' actions. They are separate individuals, and whatever they do is just that—whatever *they* do. No one thinks of you in the same way. So laugh it off, if you can.

2. Talk to them. If what they did is too heavy to be laughed at, then you might just need to talk to them. If they yelled at you in front of everyone, then maybe it's time to talk to them alone and explain to them how that makes you feel and how you understand their anger but you'd appreciate it if next time they could save it till you got home. Remember, anger only escalates things, so be calm when you talk about this. If you want a fight, then scream and yell, but chances are you don't want a fight any more than they do, so calm down and talk like an adult. Don't let yourself get ramped up; it only makes things worse. Start a fight and not only are you embarrassed of them but you're grounded, or getting the silent treatment, or having to listen to more yelling.

What I want you to get is that you can greatly influence the outcome of situations by how you act and react. A lot of kids feel helpless when it comes to their parents. They think they have no control of the relationship, but that's just not true. How you react to them greatly affects the situation. It's hard to have a one-sided fight. So if you don't allow yourself to get loud and angry they won't have as much reason to fight. It's like this in all of life. You are 50 percent of the relationship. You want to stop the fighting, then duh, stop fighting.

3. Talk about them. Your parents might not understand that what they are doing is embarrassing you. A good way to help them get it is to talk to them about their childhood. See if you can't dig up some times when they were embarrassed by their parents. If they can sympathize with your plight, then they might actually get it and lay off a little. . . .

4. Make a list. This works in all kinds of situations. When you have no power to change the way people act, you can start to change the way you think about the people who are acting weird. Changing how you think can change how you feel, and that's your goal, after all—not to feel so embarrassed of your parents. So here's an idea: let's change the way you think about them by making a list of the good stuff about them. It can really help your mind. There are lots of good things about them; you just need to dig them up in your mind and put them down on paper to look at every time you think you're going to lose it because of the stupid stuff they do.

5. Give them time. A lot of times parents are doing stuff that embarrasses you because they just want to be closer to you. When you were little you needed them and wanted them around all the time. Now that you are getting older, you need more time to yourself. That's part of growing up, but don't forget about them. They still want your attention. So make some time for them. Do some things alone together. Go out to lunch once a week. Or go shopping. Do something that both of you like, just the two of you, so you can fill that void that they are trying to fill with their embarrassing moments.

6. Show them What Not to Wear. If they are totally out of touch in the wardrobe department, send a video to TLC's *What Not to Wear* and get them a $5,000 shopping spree. But the truth is that what they wear isn't really that important to *your* life. Remember, it has no reflection on you in your friends' eyes. But if you want to help them out and help them get up-to-date, then show them some cool stuff. Remember, they aren't kids and shouldn't be dressing like you, but there are things that can hip them up a little. Take your dad shopping. I'm sure he'd love the input and the time alone with you. Talk to your mom about fashion and trends. It can be fun to give them a "what not to wear" of their own with just you. I know my mom and I loved our times together out finding her cute clothes. Sometimes they are just too busy to take the time to find out what's cool, and other times they just don't have the skills to figure it out. So don't tell them how embarrassed you are of their clothes; just encourage them to find better stuff. . . .

Remember, as you get older, your parents are getting older too. And the thing about getting older is that once you start seeing your kid doing the fun stuff you used to do, you start to feel your age and hate it. You remember everything you could do when you were younger, and you miss it. The last thing you want to be is a boring *old person*. So a lot of parents make up for the uncomfortable feeling by trying to act young. Total embarrassment, I know. Why won't they just act their age? Face it, you don't like being thought of as boring or uncool, and sometimes your parents feel just the same. So they overcompensate so you and your friends won't dislike them. They have no clue it's so irritating to you.

It's not like your parents hate you and want to embarrass you wherever you go; it's just their personalities. And even though it's rough, you have to remember that you can't change anyone other than yourself. So refuse to be embarrassed. They are really no reflection on you. And half the time your friends don't see them in the same way you do. They might actually like their stupid jokes or their "hip" conversation. Just try to focus on the amazing fact that you have parents who love and protect you.

Okay, so that's what I told your kids. Now how about you? You can do some things to better the situation if you don't like the way things are going right now. Let's take a closer look at our top 10 list. If you fit into any of these categories, please give these ideas some thought. I will say that you are the parent, and you don't have to change for your teenager. Ultimately, they need to submit to your authority and learn to live in your life. But if you want things to be different and you covet a more congenial relationship, you might want to consider some lifestyle improvements, teen style.

TOP 10 Ways Parents EmBarrass Their Teenagers—anD How to Change Things

1. **Yelling at them in public—If I were going to suggest you change any one thing you're doing, I'd suggest you change this one.** When you yell at your teenager in public, you do a great deal to damage their young hearts and minds. Your goal, I assume, is to raise a confident, successful person, and yelling at them and belittling them in public is a surefire way to create a weak, depressed, and dysfunctional adult. If yelling has to happen, it can be saved for in private. My vote is that it rarely has to happen at all. You usually yell because you feel powerless, and that shows your teenager that you are out of control. **If they are going to manipulate anyone, it is going to be the parent who shows their weakness. So maintain your composure.** If you feel like you're going to explode, you should excuse yourself, take a break, and talk to them when you are more in control. Yelling at them in public teaches your child that disrespect is an accepted behavior. The more you yell, the more things ramp up—and the more disrespect you may see out of your teenager.

Consistency is key with children of all ages. But teens are especially aware of your inconsistency and weaknesses. When you tell them you are going to do something, either negative or positive, and you don't follow through on it, they are taking note. And the next time you promise something, whether it's punishment or favor, they will be less likely to believe you. And if you're using idle threats as leverage to get them to do something, don't be surprised if they don't make an impact. Follow through on what you say you are going to do when you say you're going to do it, and your teen will be more likely to respect your word.

2. **Dressing less than fashionably**—This is a hard one. You're busy; you don't have time to keep up with all the fashions and shop till you drop. I understand, but **if you are still wearing clothes you bought more than ten years ago, you might just be causing your fashion-conscious teen to blush.** It's true that we shouldn't judge a book by its cover, and judging appearances is so superficial, but it's how we think as human beings. In my book *Sexy Girls: How Hot Is Too Hot?* I tell girls that everyone who leaves the house each day is sending a message by how they dress, and that message is your own personal marketing campaign. Whether you realize it or not, how you dress tells people how you want them to think of you. So if you would like some more respect or even just a friendlier response from your kids, take a second look at your marketing campaign. Does it say, "I'm clueless about the twenty-first century and still live in the 1980s," or does it say, "I understand what my 'look' communicates, and I'm not clueless like you might think I am." Clothes really do make the person, so do your kid a favor and spruce up your wardrobe. Here are some pointers:

Update Your Wardrobe—What Not to Wear:

· **Jeans—**If you are still wearing jeans you wore more than ten years ago, I guarantee you look out-of-date. Jeans are forever changing and forever telling the world what era you live in. So ask your teen to go shopping with you and find some more appropriate bottoms to bring you into the land of the living.

· **Patterns—**You love colors, especially lots of them. But if you are wearing busy prints, you might be calling un-needed attention to yourself that is embarrassing your teenager. Calm things down by doing more solids and less busy patterns. Solids are a safer bet when it comes to looking more like someone your kids would be proud to be seen with.

· **Fabric—**Polyester out, natural fabrics in! Go through your closet and throw out all your "wears like iron" polyester clothes. For teenagers, clothes aren't about durability; they're about appeal. As long as you dress like a geek, teenagers are going to treat you like a geek. So if you want to make your child feel more comfortable with you around their friends, do them a favor and get rid of the granny clothes.

· **Socks—**Many a dad has been a complete embarrass-ment to their child by showing up at the church picnic in Bermuda shorts, black socks, and tennis shoes. Please, for the love of Pete and all Pete's friends, don't do it. Get rid of the dress socks or knee-highs when wearing shorts. Push them down or don't wear any at all. Heck, try flip-flops—they're cheap and all the rage.

Clothes aren't the most important thing in the world, but relating to your teen is pretty high on the list. If you fear that your wardrobe is causing them any kind of grief (and they are usually quick to tell you that), then do something about it if, and only if, becoming a bigger part of your teen's life is important to you. Ask them to go to the mall with you. Don't do the teen stores; stick to the big people stores, but buy things that flatter you and prove that you are on the ball. Your teen will thank you for it. And your relationship will improve.

3. **Trying to be "cool"**—A lot of parents hate the fact that they are getting older, and in order to forget it or to hide it, they act like teenagers themselves. Or at least they try. Now, there's nothing wrong with having a really cool mom or dad. But that means a parent who isn't embarrassing and who is kind, friendly, non-invasive, and loving. It doesn't mean a parent who dresses and talks like they're still twenty-two. **If you find yourself trying to entertain your kid's friends or spending every weekend with the gang, then perhaps you're trying too hard to be the kid and not the parent.** All teenagers want their parent to do is to be the parent. That means you listen to their stories, you talk to them about their life, but you don't try to infiltrate it or make their circle of friends your own. Teenagers want a parent who is there for them but not trying too hard to be liked. Remember, your job is not to be liked but to be the adult. Don't make the mistake of thinking that a cool parent is better than an available parent. There's a difference. Be available to drive them, talk to them, and help them, but don't force yourself into their lives. They are on the journey to adulthood and want and need to be themselves, make their own friends, and keep you as their parent.

4. **Being too loud and drawing attention to yourself and them**—This is often closely related to wanting to be "cool." Loud parents are an embarrassment because they are

trying to draw all of the attention to themselves. This makes the child feel like they are being either upstaged or humiliated. When you draw attention to yourself by being loud, you are really saying to your child and the world, "It's all about me! What about me? I need some attention." That's something we expect from a four-year-old, not an adult. Now, that doesn't mean you become a church mouse around your kids; what it means is that if your kids are noticeably embarrassed by your antics out in public, dial it back a notch until you get home. You don't have to change who you are—just put it on hold.

5. **Being too affectionate in public**—When they were little they loved your hugs and kisses, and now it seems to pain them. What happened? Did they suddenly stop loving you? No, they actually started growing up. Adolescence is the time when kids are exploring the world. They are learning how to function as individuals, and when you are overly affectionate, you make them feel, and look to their friends, like a little baby. For a teen who is learning to grow up and fend for themselves, this is a huge embarrassment. It says to their friends that they are still babies and need the constant coddling of their parents—or at least that's what they feel it means. So save the affection for the privacy of your home, and help them make the giant step into adulthood by giving them their space in public.

6. **Treating them like a little kid in front of their friends**— When your child was a baby, you would spit on your fingers and wipe their face because they couldn't do it themselves. But when you do that and other babying-type things now, you make them feel like they aren't big enough to care for themselves. And as I've been saying, this is the time

in your child's life when they need to practice leaving the nest and flying solo. If they can't take care of themselves now, then how will they ever do it when they are truly out on their own? So control yourself. Resist the urge to treat them like they are a kid in front of their friends.

7. **Grilling their girlfriend or boyfriend**—This one is totally understandable. When your teenager has a date, it's good for you to know who they are dating. I don't want to tell you not to do this, but it can really embarrass your teenager. Frankly, I think it's something they're just going to have to learn to live with, although there might be ways of doing it that are, say, more sympathetic than other ways. But if you have a daughter, more often than not your teen has given you too few minutes between the doorbell ringing and the time their movie starts to have a "normal" conversation with your daughter's new crush. Someone is going to feel grilled. Even though your teen would like me to tell you to stop, stop, stop this, I just can't do it.

8. **Saying something stupid in front of their friends**—This one is almost unavoidable . . . at least I know it is for me! Sometimes you're going to put your foot in your mouth, no matter who you're with. Just do your best not to be too unguarded with your word selection in front of the friends.

9. **Drinking too much or doing drugs**—This one seems obvious to most, but some parents feel like they have a right to keep on doing the things they've always done, including

mood-altering substances. If this is you, I encourage you to get help. If you want successful teens who will always be there for you and even care for you in your old age, then consider the fact that if you continue to abuse drugs or alcohol, you will more than likely soon be estranged from your teen, who is at great risk of taking on the same behavior as you.

10. **Not taking care of your body**—No one said parenting was easy, so why would you be shocked that it might also include taking better care of yourself? Giving your child the gift of your health is priceless. If your body draws attention to your teenager, then I can almost guarantee you that they are embarrassed. Teens desperately hope to avoid situations that will make them look odd, and that includes having an odd parent. If your appearance is beyond your control, then your teen will have to learn to thrive in the face of potential embarrassment. But if it's something that you can easily change by buying new glasses or a cane instead of a walker, or just using more deodorant then you might want to give it a try. If you are dangerously overweight, the issue is not just you being an embarrassment to your body-conscious teen but the fact that you are increasing your chances of many diseases and disabilities.

In *Stupid Parents* I tell your teens that your look isn't anything for them to be ashamed of, so don't get me wrong here. I'm not blaming you or telling you that you must change or hide out in order to ease the pain of their embarrassment. I'm only suggesting that if there is something about you that is changeable, would benefit you, and would make life easier for your teenager, you might want to give change a try. And who knows, you might end up feeling better about yourself as well.

Ideas to Consider

The embarrassing question—Ask your teenager to tell you their most embarrassing moment. If it doesn't involve you, listen to the story, and then ask them to tell you one time *you* embarrassed them. Be sure to listen—don't argue or get mad. This is an exercise in self-improvement for you, and you can't ask and then blow up at them. Remember, you're the adult here, and your goal is to better your relationship with your child.

After you find out how you embarrassed them, spend some time by yourself thinking about the situation. Can you understand why they felt the way they did? How does it make you feel? Would you like to make sure it doesn't happen again? Then take the necessary steps to make sure it doesn't. Embarrassments happen, but with a little understanding and self-analysis, you can make them more rare and improve your child's life.

The Overprotective Parent

When your child was a baby, you had to guard their every move. You baby-proofed the house and kept a watchful eye on them. You turned the pot handles so they didn't hang over the front of the stove, and you taught your child the meaning of "no." But as they've gotten older, they've started to become more and more independent, and now suddenly they want to do everything on their own. In fact, they are starting to push the limits. They want to stay out later and later; they want to choose their own friends, dress the way *they* want, and decide what and when they'll eat and where they'll go. And your blood pressure and stress level are going up. You want to be a good parent; you want your kids to learn discipline, to be safe, to not make big mistakes. But at what point do you become overprotective?

As your kids enter their teen years, they start the often-painful process of leaving the nest. Empty-nest syndrome is a well-known ache that many parents face when their kids have all grown up and moved out. But I think for many parents another syndrome hits before the child actually leaves the house. I call it **"my baby has grown up" syndrome.** It's hard on a lot of parents who long for the days of baby and hugs and cuddles. But the truth is that all of us must grow up. We can't stay little all our lives. And adolescence is where you notice this the most. **The teen years are essentially the time when your child is beginning to take practice flights out of the nest.** They stretch their wings and test the winds to see how well they can handle life on their own. This is normal and necessary for children to pass from adolescence to adulthood. But the truth is that many young people aren't being allowed to grow up.

I have a baby who just learned to walk. My husband, Michael, and I have strategically placed all the furniture to inflict the least amount of pain when fallen into. It's hard to watch your baby walk around like a drunk sailor within inches of sharp corners, hard tables, and feisty pets, but after taking all the normal precautions, the only alternative would be to never let her walk. But we all know it has to happen. She has to walk and fall down, bump her head and bite her lip. Accidents will happen, and we work with that. The same goes for your teenager. You can do all you can to make their life safe, but in the end you have to let them learn to walk on their own. They have to be expected to break your favorite lamp, put the first scratch on your car, fail at things, and get hurt—otherwise they'll never learn to walk independently from you.

When you are overprotective with your teenager, you are essentially telling them you don't trust them. That does a couple things to their thought life. One is that it just makes them mad; they feel like they're wearing a straightjacket, and it's exasperating. It can also cause them to feel unsure, to doubt themselves, because they don't have a track record of life on their own. A phenomenon is sweeping the nation and the world: teens who aren't compelled to grow up and manage their own lives are opting to delay adulthood longer and longer. This has become such a popular life choice that sociologists have even started to name it—*adultescence* is one I prefer. It's adults living and acting like kids for years and years after adolescence. It might seem harmless at first, but the impact on society and your family will most definitely take its toll.

The Kidult

Our society is full of lost boys and girls hanging out at the edge of adulthood. Yet we find it difficult even to give them a name. The absence of a readily recognized word to describe these infantilized adults demonstrates the unease with which this phenomenon is greeted. Advertisers and toy manufacturers have invented the term "kidult" to describe this segment of the market. Another word sometimes used to describe these 20- to 35-year-olds is "adultescent," generally defined as someone who refuses to settle down and make commitments, and who would rather go on partying into middle age.

Stephanie K. Taylor, "Delaying Adulthood," *Washington Times*, August 16, 2003.

The Thirty-Year-Old Little Boy

More than a few parents must be puzzled by the reluctance of their twentysomething children to leave home. Look at poor Giuseppe Andreoli, an anatomy professor at Naples University and a former member of the Italian parliament. In 2002, the Italian courts ruled that he must continue to pay his thirty-year-old son Marco £500 per month until he found satisfactory employment. Marco lived with his mother and was in no hurry to fly the nest. The judge felt that Andreoli continued to have responsibility for his son's maintenance until Marco found a job worthy of his own "aspirations."

Philip Willan, "Italian court tells father to support stay-at-home son, 30," *Guardian*, April 6, 2002.

This might not be your dilemma right now, but many parents are being faced with their twentysomething kids not wanting to leave home. It might seem nice to have them around, but the truth is that you aren't doing them any good. This lack of ability to accept responsibility and move into the next phase of life is stunting not only the child but the family. **More and more young people are choosing to remain kids rather than forming independent lives of their own.** An entire book could be written on this subject, so I'll save my ideas for that, but let me just leave you with the idea that if you really are being overprotective and not encouraging your child to accept responsibility and the arrival of adulthood, you may just be helping to create a generation of lazy, infantile adults who are failing to step up to the plate and carry the torch of the previous generation.

That said, I'm sure it's not your goal to *over*protect your child, but just in case you are overprotecting, here's what you and your teen need to know.

BuilDing ResPonsiBility

I believe we all want our kids to be responsible, and that requires that they learn responsibility. In other words, they must have things they are tasked with doing and will have to give an account of or answer for. I like the definition of *responsible* that says, "able to choose for oneself between right and wrong." **If you want your teenager to choose rightly, then you have to give them the chance to choose and accept the fact that they might choose differently than you.** Forcing your child to always choose what you consider to be right is a surefire way to teach them to choose wrongly when they are away from you. The way your child thinks is this: *If you are going to force your decisions on me, then I can't wait till I'm away from you so I can explore the opposite for myself.* Teens want and need to be taught decision making by their parents. But after you teach them, you have to allow them to move out and practice making decisions on their own. That's not only how you build reliable and healthy adults but also how you create a warm and loving relationship at home.

One of the biggest ways that parents overprotect their teens and fail to teach them about responsibility is with regard to cause and effect. If your teenager comes home with a bad grade and whines to you about how bad the teacher is and how she has something against him, you have two options. You can either side with your child and call the teacher to do all you can to remove him from her class or get his grade changed, or you can teach your child about living and thriving under authority. The way you do the latter is by teaching him that he will always have someone over him who has the final say—a boss, the government, the police. And unless he learns how best to relate to these people, you will be forever bailing him out of trouble.

Teenagers need to learn that their actions have consequences and that oftentimes the actions of others also have consequences that we have to learn to live with. When parents continue to fight for their kids into the teen and twentysomething years, they create whiney, self-entitled pseudo-adults who are too weak to succeed on their own in the competitive world. But if you allow your child to work their way out of their own fixes, they will grow stronger and stronger as individuals and be able to manage the rough terrain of life on their own.

Overprotected and Pampered Demographic Definitions

Parasite single or stay-at-home adult—a single adult who still lives at home with their parents

Kidult—a young person, age twenty to thirty, who refuses to grow up

Adultescence—the age between twenty and thirty when people who should be adults are still playing games and acting like kids, refusing to accept responsibility

Singletons—people in their twenties and thirties who choose not to make relationship commitments involving marriage and family (I know of which I speak, I was one!)

*Stephanie Taylor, "Delaying Adulthood," *Washington Times*, August 16, 2003.

It's quite a trend now for parents to be very active in their young adults' college lives—calling teachers, meeting with counselors—and it might seem like a responsible thing to do. But it softens the mind of your young adult and keeps them as children. Now their first response is not problem solving but telephoning you to fix things. Dr. Frank Furedi, professor of sociology at the University of Kent at Canterbury in England, tells parents that such an **extended dependence on parents reflects a "fear of adulthood" in the culture at large.** Adulthood has become "something that you want to distance yourself from. Adulthood is no longer seen as having positive attributes."* What a tragedy. Adulthood is inevitable and should be something that is coveted. But instead we are protecting our young people from it and creating a generation of weaklings. If you want to help your teenager mature and succeed, practice letting go while they are still at home and allowing them to learn to live with consequences. That's the best way for a young person to learn responsibility.

Just to clarify, I'm not advocating a complete abandonment of Junior. I'm not suggesting you never come to his aid. Of course at times he will need your help, but I encourage you and your spouse to discuss each scenario and determine if it is better for your child's development to learn to work it out on his own or to be rescued by you.

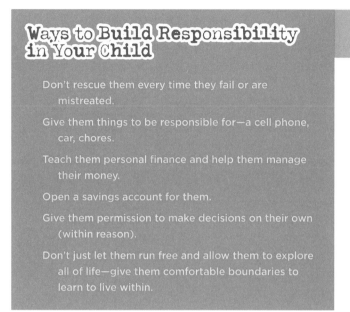

Ways to Build Responsibility in Your Child

Don't rescue them every time they fail or are mistreated.

Give them things to be responsible for—a cell phone, car, chores.

Teach them personal finance and help them manage their money.

Open a savings account for them.

Give them permission to make decisions on their own (within reason).

Don't just let them run free and allow them to explore all of life—give them comfortable boundaries to learn to live within.

The Opposite of Overprotective

Some parents overreact to the "overprotective" label and allow their kids to do whatever they want, whenever they want. Let me just tell you that for the developing mind of a teenager, this is just as dangerous as you being overprotective. It gives the young person no boundaries and instead forces them to find truth and define morality on their own, without the wisdom of parents. Though some teens might jump at the chance, watch out, because you could end up with a child who acts the same as one who is overprotected. He very likely will become lazy and disassociated with life, because teens tend to take the easy route when given the chance. So don't overcorrect your overprotection and take off all limits. Just move the borders of their limits out bit by bit as they prove themselves to you more and more each day.

One of the major jobs of teenagers is to start becoming more and more their own person. That means they don't need their parents as much, they start making decisions on their own, and they learn to handle the consequences that go along with those decisions. Some parents miss this crucial fact: kids have to grow up. And you have to trust that you've raised them well enough to do that. But how does "grown up" look? How do you know when your teenager is ready to start making their own decisions? Well, here are a few things I told teens in *Stupid Parents* that I would encourage you to take as progress if you see them implemented in their lives. If your child can address these issues, then maybe you, the overprotective parent, can make some advancement toward allowing them more space. When they understand their responsibility and you understand their need for it, then you both can become much happier. Here's what I told them.

1. **Agree with them.** The best thing to do with an over-protective parent is to let them know that you understand their concerns. If you argue with them and tell them that it's stupid for them to worry about you going to the mall alone, they are going to continue to think that you are just too young to understand things. The key is to let them know that you get it. You are concerned about protecting yourself too; they aren't alone. Let them know you realize how dangerous it can be when you're at the mall with just your friends. Tell them that you know all about protecting yourself—not walking out to the car alone, not getting in a car with strangers, etc. Whatever it is that they talk about being fearful of, let them know that you totally agree, that

stuff is dangerous, and that's why you take so much care to avoid it. When you agree with them rather than argue with them, they will slowly start to see your "maturity." And as that happens, they can start to feel more free to loosen the grip because they know that you have it all under control.

2. **Accept responsibility.** If you want them to treat you like an adult, then you have to start to move more toward your independence. That means you have to start to take responsibility for yourself and your actions. Things like cleaning up after yourself show a degree of maturity and independence. I mean, little kids need their parents to pick up after them and cook their meals. An adult can do those things on their own without whining about it. If you make a mistake, own up to it. That's a true sign of your ability to be mature and independent. If you run to your parents to fix things you do wrong or trouble you get into, then you aren't exactly encouraging them to loosen up and let you do the things you want to do. The more you can do to show how responsible you are, the more likely they are to let you do the things you want to do.

Show Them You Can Be Trusted

Parents are overprotective because they worry that you can't take care of yourself. Your first order of business is to prove to them that you *can* be trusted. This is going to take some time, but it's the only way that you can get them to trust you and stop being so overprotective. Here are some basic ways.

1. **Don't hide things from them.** If they feel like you are hiding stuff, then they are more likely to try to control your life in order to protect you. So don't be all secretive. Keep your door open. Invite them into your room to talk. Share stuff with them, like your favorite music or hobby or

In the USA singletons are the fastest growing demographic group. The proportion of households containing one person increased by nine percent between 1970 and 2000.

Frank Furedi, "The Children Who Won't Grow Up," July 29, 2003, http://www.spiked-online.com/Articles/00000006DE8D.htm.

whatever is unique to you. Make them a part of your life, and they'll be less likely to worry about you because they'll feel they know you inside and out.

2. **Introduce them to your friends.** The more they get to know your friends, the more they can trust you with them. If you have friends they don't know, they might start to imagine all kinds of horrible things you guys are doing together. An informed parent is a more relaxed parent.

3. **Apologize.** If you mess up and do something stupid or against the rules, apologize quickly. Agree with them that you were wrong and explain why you did what you did. Help them to understand that as you grow up, you will do more and more things independently, but they can trust you because you know the dangers out there and you know how to be careful.

My So-Called Online Life

With kids so into things like personal webpages, blogs, and social networking sites like MySpace.com, parents have a whole new category of paranoia. All you hear about are the horror stories of kids being in danger online. How can you protect them? Get involved. In *Stupid Parents* I asked your teenager to get online with you and show you what they do, where they go, and who their "friends" are. You can get involved in their Internet life just like you get involved in the rest of their life. But remember, you have to be able to trust them. If you are convinced they are smart and understand danger signs, then you don't have to look over their shoulder all the time they are online. For more control, don't let them have a computer in their room. Keep it in the family room or kitchen—somewhere where they can't hide what they're doing. A responsible and smart kid is one who isn't afraid for you to see their world. Just don't go overboard.

Better Safe Than Sorry

Below is a list I shared with your teenager in *Stupid Parents*. Girls especially need to understand how predators think and the ways to avoid becoming a victim. I don't want them to be fearful, but they do need to be prepared. Look over the list and discuss it with your daughter. My mom taught me this as a matter of fact, not as a scare tactic, and I never forgot all her wisdom. Taking these precautions only takes moments of your life but can save you a world of hurt.

1. Make it hard on them. If a robber asks for your wallet and/or purse, *don't reach out and hand it to him*! Toss it away from you. More than likely he's more interested in

it than you, and he will go for it. *When he does, run like mad in the other direction while screaming.*

2. Get seen. If you are ever thrown into the trunk of a car, kick out the back taillights, stick your arm out the hole, and start waving like crazy. The driver won't see you, but everybody else will. You can also look for the glow-in-the-dark trunk release tab and pull it. Or move toward the front of the car and push on the back of the backseats to see if they release into the car.

3. Lock the doors. Girls especially tend to get into our cars after shopping, eating, working, etc., and start putting on lip gloss or digging for our phones. *Don't do this!* The bad guy will be watching you, and this is the perfect opportunity for him to get in on the passenger side, put a gun to your head, and tell you where to go. *As soon as you get into the car, lock the doors and leave.*

4. Don't go with them. If someone is in your car with a gun to your head, *do not drive off with them!* Instead, gun the engine and speed into anything you can, wrecking the car. Your air bag will save you. If the person is in the backseat, they will get the worst of it. As soon as the car crashes, bail out and run. It is better than having them find your body in a remote location. Another idea is to drive to the police station rather than where he asks you. Remind him that if he shoots you the car will wreck and he'll get hurt.

5. Tips for when getting into your car in a parking lot or parking garage:

   Be aware: look around you and look into your car at the passenger side floor and in the backseat.

   Avoid the van. If you are parked next to a big van, enter your car from the passenger door. An abductor can easily pull you into their van while you're getting into your car.

Don't go it alone. Look at the car parked on the driver's side of your vehicle. If a male is sitting alone in the seat nearest your car (on the passenger side), you may want to walk back into the mall or your workplace and get a guard or policeman to walk you back out.

It's always better to be safe than sorry. (And better paranoid than dead.)

6. No stairs. *Always* take the elevator instead of the stairs. Stairwells are horrible places to be alone and the perfect crime spot. This is especially true at night.

7. Stay out. If there is just one guy in the elevator, say, "I'll wait for the next one." You don't want to be alone in a small space with a potential bad guy.

8. Run. If the bad guy has a gun and you can run, *always run!* The bad guy will have a much harder time of hitting a moving target, and even if he does hit you, it most likely *will not* be a vital organ. Run in a zigzag pattern—that makes you the hardest to hit.

9. Let somebody else help them. Girls, don't be sympathetic to strangers. It can get you raped or killed. Ted Bundy, the serial killer, was a good-looking, well-educated guy who *always* played on the sympathies of unsuspecting women. He walked with a cane or a limp and often asked for help getting into his car or with his car, which was when he abducted his victims.

Setting the GrounD Rules

Negotiating with teenagers can drive parents crazy, but as long as there are rules, there will be negotiations. And that's not such a bad thing. When you teach your child to negotiate, you teach them a valuable life skill. So rather than arguing with them, lay the ground rules for negotiation, keeping in mind that you are giving them tools for their future.

First, always be clear as to the ground rules. Talk with them often about what is in and out of bounds. Make a list of absolutes—the things you are guaranteed never to compromise on. For example, what do you expect from them when it comes to parties, dates, or group activities? Do you expect phone calls or conversations with other parents? Make a list of requirements and talk it over with them so there isn't any arguing the key issues that you will not compromise on. But remember, if you can leave some things open for discussion and compromise, then you can teach your child the give-and-take of negotiations.

For example, let's say your rule is no rock concerts. Your daughter is fifteen, and you don't want her going to music venues with her friends. She knows that, but one of her good friends is performing at a coffee shop in the city. She comes to you and asks if she can go. You say no. She refuses to give up and says, "What about . . ." and before she can finish, your hand is up and you are yelling, "No! No concerts!" You've just skipped over the art of negotiation and missed a valuable opportunity to teach her critical thinking and compromise. So hear her out. She might say, "What about if you go with me and my friends and sit at the coffee bar while we listen?" Voila! Negotiation at its finest. Wow, now you have to give her credit for wanting something and figuring out how to get it. You might be busy that day, but I say drop what you're doing and go with her. It will build her confidence in herself and in you.

Consider the Options

If your child really wants to do or have something you are not willing to allow, ask them to spend some time thinking of options that you might approve of. Ask them to go off and think and then put into writing some viable options. The ground rules have to be that you have the final say and you can veto any of their ideas. Talk about a great way to teach them to live under authority! Don't get angry if their options don't sit right with you. Listen intently, and then discuss the viability of each. If you want to grow their wisdom and negotiating skills, avoid arguments and belittling their thoughts. Give them credit for creativity, and make your determination. The more you do this, the more they will know you and your rules.

In interpersonal relationships as well as business, flexibility is key. The more you can show your ability to be convinced by your child, the more you will increase the frequency and openness of communication at home.

Ideas to Consider

Building responsibility—It's time to let go of your baby and allow them to learn to walk on their own and, yes, even to fall down. You are always there to pick them up, but you must let them go. You don't have to do it all at once, but you've got to do it. Find ways that you can allow them more and more responsibility. Remember that each time you do, you are equipping them for adulthood. Find something they are interested in doing and let them do it. Feel free to give ground rules, but if you are an overprotective parent who is afraid to let them grow up, you have to break the cycle and take the plunge of letting go. Each time they master a new skill or responsibility, allow them more freedom. The more responsibility you can give them, the healthier and happier their lives will be both with and without you.

Negotiation 101—Make sure you've given your child a clear understanding of the rules you want them to live under. Spend some time thinking about what you will and won't allow and why. Then make a list of things that are off-limits to your child. Find a time when they are available to sit for a while and talk about your list. Don't just give them a laundry list; talk it over with them like a boss would do with a new employee. Allow them to ask the question "But why?" and try your best to give a better answer than "Because I said so." But if all else fails, that's a valid response. You are, after all, the one responsible for their lives. Teach them about negotiations and let them know you are up for discussing whatever they come up with, but the ground rules are that there will be no yelling, arguing, or whining. Treat it like a business, and help them to understand that logic will win out over raw emotion.

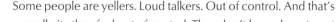

Why All the Yelling?

Some people are yellers. Loud talkers. Out of control. And that's really it—they feel out of control. They don't know how to get other people to do what they want, so they think that if they yell, they can get through to them better. It's like the foreigner who doesn't speak the language trying to ask for directions. He thinks that if he talks louder, somehow the person will understand him. It's just human nature. The more we think someone isn't listening or doesn't understand us, the louder we tend to get. That doesn't make it right or even make it better; it's just the way it seems to be.

But what about at home? **Do you have a yelling problem?** Do you feel that the only way you can get your child's attention is to be louder? That's not always the case. The teen mind has a keen ability to toggle-task. They used to call it multitasking, but the truth is that the mind can't do more than one thing at a time. But when we're young, we can toggle from task to task at breakneck speeds. What this means to you is that your child has the ability to toggle right on past you and your yelling. They can close you out with more than a door. Being ignored can be frustrating, so you yell even louder. In some cases, they choose not to ignore you, and the fight is on.

Let me just say that yelling at a teenager or any child doesn't get you anywhere. **Teens are smart; they understand that when you yell, you are trying to maintain the power that you feel slipping out of your fingers.** And that signals weakness. The parent to be reckoned with is the one who doesn't lose control and end up yelling. In the teenager's eyes, the strong parent is the one who refuses to be the child and get emotional. That's the parent who knows that ultimately they are in control and so feels no need to waste the energy yelling.

When dealing with a teenager, it's important to understand that you aren't dealing with your baby anymore. When they were young, the yelling might have scared them, gotten their attention, and showed them who was the boss. (Not that I am condoning yelling at younger children; I find it futile with any age. But I want to help you understand the difference in the teenager's mind.) The teenager has a different level of development. They are almost adults. They make critical decisions and can think for themselves, but their minds and emotions are in flux. And that's why yelling can have such an adverse effect on them. Coming home to yelling is like coming home to a war zone for your teen.

For the boy who is attempting to learn how to become a man, yelling can make him feel emasculated. Teenage boys are at a crucial developmental stage where they are pulling away from you in an effort to establish their independence. They tend to hide out a lot and find ways to distance themselves, especially from their mothers. That is because of their emerging sexuality and the confusion that can be created with mom and her femininity. In other words, as a boy's sexuality starts to blossom he may become uncomfortable showing physical affection with his mother, because he begins to see all women as sexual beings and "mom hugs" get confusing. And as boys are exploring their manhood, yelling can be a huge deterrent in this development, making them angry and driving them into more and more isolation. Your teenage boy can take your yelling as a threat to his masculinity. No wonder he yells back to prove his dominance or disappears to establish his independence. If you want to raise a healthy boy, then stop the yelling at all costs. It does nothing but break down the man he is on the way to becoming.

For girls the situation is slightly different. Girls are emotionally charged. Their hormones are playing tricks with their hearts and their minds, and a constant barrage of yelling can cause them much emotional and mental confusion. Different girls deal with yelling in different ways. Some of them will take it as an insult to who they are and internalize messages like, "I'm not worth anything. No one loves me. I'm not beautiful." Of course you aren't saying any of this, but their little hearts are in upheaval and tend to assign drastic notions to small things. Other girls might feel less of a pull to the emotional and instead deal with your yelling by expressing their own anger and rage. Either way, yelling turns a vulnerable girl into a victim of her emotions. Teaching your daughter to make decisions and react based on what's right and not what feels right is your biggest task. And when you lose control and yell, you teach her that acting on emotion is an acceptable way of life. If you act on emotion and lose control, you can't be surprised when she loses control as well.

Yelling never accomplishes what you want it to accomplish. Sure, it may help you let off a little steam, but in the process you create such strife and anger in the home that you only end up making things worse. The trouble with yelling is that the more you do it, the more you and your family become desensitized to it. First you yell to get their attention, then they get used to your yelling, so you yell more, and it just keeps getting worse and worse. So the next time you want to yell or you face a child who is yelling, refuse to give in. Count to ten. Remove yourself. Do whatever it takes to remain the grown-up. Teaching your children how to manage their emotions is one of the greatest gifts you can give them.

Here's what I told your teen to do when you're yelling:

1. Don't yell back.

2. Talk calmly.

3. Give them a hug.

4. Stop whatever you are doing that is making them mad.

5. Listen.

Ideas to consider

Stop the yelling—Talk to your teenager about the ways you talk to each other. Ask them if they think you yell too much and how it makes them feel. Use this as an opportunity to apologize and to tell them that you want to change. Ask them to agree with you that the yelling should stop, and then work together to come up with some ways to curb it next time it happens. Here are some ideas you can play with:

- Come up with an escape word. Agree on a word to use when one of you realizes the argument is getting out of control. Saying this word means, "Let's stop, take a deep breath, and reconvene when we've calmed down." Make it a word that doesn't usually come up in conversation, like *architecture* or *longitude*. When one of you says that word, you both stop talking and take a break.

- Another way to stop the yelling is to learn to take turns talking. Oftentimes we yell because the other person is talking over us and can't hear us. That's unhealthy communication. Come up with something, like a timer, a rock, or a bowl, that you will pass back and forth. Whoever has ahold of the item is allowed to talk; the other person must listen. But there is a time limit. Each person can only talk for two minutes before they have to pass the baton. This allows both of you to feel heard, and that helps cut the need to yell.

- Experiment with whatever methods you need to use in order to stop yelling. Count to ten, go outside, do anything in order to stop yelling. Remember, whatever you're yelling about is never as important as the love and respect of your teenager. Things always change, and your teen will one day work through whatever it is you are struggling with. Sometimes you just have to trust the parenting you've done up to this point.

Emotion Overload

Oh, the drama. Sometimes it seems like your teenager can make a mountain out of a grain of sand. She dramatizes everything: "He didn't smile at me. How could he?" "She said I was fat—I want to die!" And the saga goes on and on. For parents it can be really hard to listen to the goofy stuff they take so seriously and not laugh or tell them to just get over it. After all, you know it will pass. You know they'll get over him. You know that the pain won't last forever. You've been there, done that. So why can't they just get over it?

I completely understand why you feel that way. And **as your child's teacher of life, you need to help them understand when something isn't that big a deal and that they will get over it.** But sometimes when you attempt just that, you make them mad. What you say and what they hear are two different things. You say, "It will get better"; they hear, "Your feelings don't matter." You say, "Rub some dirt on it"; they hear, "I don't care how you feel." **When hormones are raging and brains are still growing, teenagers' minds can play tricks on them.** And those who love them can look like those who hate them. Let me just tell you, it will get better, and all you have to do is rub some dirt on it. I promise, this too shall pass. But meanwhile, how do you live with the ever-changing mind and emotions of a teenager? **What can you do to ease the strife of the emotionally charged mind?**

Listen

The most important thing your teenager wants when they whine and complain is two ears. **They just want someone to listen. They don't necessarily want it fixed;** they just want to voice it and live it over again—especially girls. Girls can get very angry when you try to fix it while they're still trying to process it. **They feel like they want time to feel bad.** So let them talk, cry, moan, and so on without telling them to stop. Let them get it out, and then you'll have a better chance at being heard.

Boys, on the other hand, tend not to share all the gory details with you or ask for your opinion until they've exhausted all other options. **To ask for help or an opinion is often considered a sign of weakness for a boy.** So don't pester your son to talk to you about his feelings. And don't be surprised when all he wants to do is to be alone in his room. Nothing is wrong with him; he is just male. And boys, just like men, like to work things out on their own. It makes them feel capable. When it comes time to actually listen to your son, you can be sure he's already given things some thought. So don't be too quick to correct him or scold him. Remember that making decisions is a skill he has to learn in order to be a grown-up. Encourage the process. Give him advice only when he asks for it, if at all possible. If you chase after him trying to help, you will more than likely just feel frustrated, and you run the risk of emasculating him or keeping him a baby.

So listen differently to your teens. Understanding who they are as individuals and how they think will help you better teach them to manage their feelings.

Q aND A

After you hear them out, ask them questions. With girls this can open a floodgate, but asking questions and waiting for their answers can help them work through their turmoil. For the most part girls are best soothed by sympathy, empathy, and understanding. But along with those "I bet you must feel awful" statements, you can throw in some lessons on wisdom. Help them understand that things will get better and that how they think about things is what impacts them, not the actual events themselves.

Try giving them books on the topics they are dealing with. The topic of boys is always a big one for girls, so help them understand how boys think. I cowrote a book called *Dateable* to do just that. I found that most of the emotional problems in teens' lives stem from relating to the opposite sex, and so *Dateable* was written to help kids better understand how the ones they are interested in think and react to them. Sometimes when they get the truth from someone other than their parent, they take it more to heart. It's a sad but true fact. So find people who can say what you're thinking in a way that will resonate with your kids. Girls for the most part love to read and will readily accept "self-help" books as a way to better themselves. If you have a daughter who turns up her nose at "your" books, then don't hand them to her. Just put it out where she can see them, and if the cover and the topic interest her, you can be sure she'll pick it up.

The important thing to remember is to validate their emotions before you give them advice. Empathize first, and they will be much more likely to listen to your words of encouragement or direction.

Boys are a bit different when it comes to the Q and A. When he comes to the point of needing to ask you for advice, you can be sure he's already given the problem a lot of thought and has run out of options or has come to a decision but wants to test it against your advice before he leaps into action. **He doesn't need empathy as much as he covets respect for trying to make a good decision.** If you can respect his thought process and tell him so, and then offer bits of advice to help him better craft his own response to the situation, he'll be more likely to accept your help and ask for more in the future. The key to remember with boys is that just like men, they crave respect and a sense that you find them capable. So do your best to exhibit trust in their decisions and to allow them to make their own mistakes.

Change the Subject

After you've listened well, had some Q and A time, and given them the time they need to feel their pain, so to speak, I suggest changing the subject. **Don't do it to be rude but to encourage them to stop ruminating on the problem and to redirect their thoughts to something more pleasurable.** Take them out for ice cream or a run. Go outside and throw a ball around. Do something with them that they enjoy so that they can learn how to redirect their thoughts to something more positive when dealing with turmoil. You will do your child a great deal of good if you can teach them to think on things that are positive rather than negative and to be content in any situation, whether well fed or hungry, whether in a happy relationship or alone in the world. Teaching your child to control their thought life is one of the most valuable gifts you can give them.

No Disrespect

Sometimes when teens get emotional, they get disrespectful. Their tempers run short, and they have little patience with your cluelessness. But **allowing your teenager to be rude or disrespectful just because they are hurt or going through something isn't doing them any favors.** So let your child vent and share, but draw the line at angry outbursts or cruel or nasty speech. They need to learn to manage themselves around others even when they aren't feeling good. When we allow them to tear into us or treat us differently when they are down, we teach them bad relational habits for school, the workplace, and even other relationships.

I am writing this book as a teen expert, not a parenting expert. So **I can say that from your teen's perspective, when you don't allow them to disrespect you, they can feel frustrated.** They don't feel like they have control of their emotions and sometimes their mouth, so it seems unfair that you are disciplining them for something they don't feel they can control. This can erupt into major turmoil. Understanding this can help you when you lay down the law. You know your child and the kind of training they need in order to function well in society, so don't let them fall apart when they have an emotional meltdown. But do consider their feeling of loss of control and try to find creative ways to validate that feeling as well as help them to manage it better. Don't expect them to get it right the first time, and don't erupt to the same level they do when they blow up on you. Stay calm. Do all the things we've talked about till now and remain the grown-up. But if they aren't being civil, then attend to that discipline problem before empathizing or asking questions anymore. In other words, don't ignore it, but don't belabor it. I think it's best to point it out, ask them to apologize, and then go on. If you find that your teen feels you disrespected them, apologize in kind. No one likes to live on a one-way street with someone who drives both ways. Don't use their disrespect as an excuse to end the conversation and get back to more important things, but do your best to maintain the respect you must have in order to be the parent.

In *Stupid Parents,* **I gave your kid four things to do when you start to help them with their emotions.** Read each point and I'll explain them to you a bit more.

> **1. Thank them.** Thank them for reminding you that "this too shall pass." Tell them you understand that you *will* get over it, even if you don't feel like it right now. Then explain to them that even though you know you'll be better, right now you just really need to feel bad. That will help you to get over it quicker. We each have our own way of dealing with things, and right now this is yours. So promise them that you will look on the bright side, remember that time

heals everything, and believe that everything will be all right—after you've had a good cry or some time alone with your game console.

This time to feel bad can't be allowed to go on and on. Allow them some time of mourning, as it were, but then **help them to get up and get on with life.** You know your child better than anyone, so you'll know when it's time to pull the plug on the drama.

> **2. Get them talking.** This one might or might not work for you, depending on your parents, but getting them talking about themselves can be a great way to get them off the subject of you and also to get them to remember how it felt to be a teenager. So ask them about the first time whatever it is that is happening to you happened to them. Ask them what they did, what their parents told them, and so on. This might not be of any concern to you at all, but it does have a way of getting them to change the subject. A lot of times all parents really need is to feel heard. They want to be validated—that is, told that they are right and that you get it and thank God for them, that kind of thing. They need to feel needed. So even if you don't feel like needing them, give it a shot. It could take the heat off and might even help you out with your situation. Best of all, it can remind them of their youth. And maybe through that they'll start to take your feelings more seriously.

This might sound like hypocrisy or condescension to you, but what I'm trying to do is to get them to go through the motions of healthy communication. **If they can do something before they feel like doing it, they are more likely to end up feeling like it.** Feelings follow action. If they will take the time to listen to you and care for you, they will not only learn from your experiences but also learn to love others as themselves. When I teach teens how to make it in communication, I first teach them what's in it for them. If they understand that listening to you will make your relationship better for them, they will be more likely to listen to you, and that's our goal here.

3. Write them a letter. If you have a hard time talking over your feelings with your parentals, then change things up and write them a letter. When someone takes the time to write something down nowadays, people have a tendency to pay more attention. You can sometimes express yourself better alone in your room with a pen and paper than you can face-to-face. So tell them your feelings and how it hurts that they don't accept that you have your own feelings, even if they do seem irrational to them. But remember, validating some of the things they've said to you in the past is a smart move. They might seem crazy to you right now or you just might believe them, but either way, you can calm your parents' frazzled fear that you're going off the deep end of emotion. Writing it all down can help clear your mind and maybe even calm your nerves.

If your child does this and hands you a note, please do what you can to stop what you are doing and read it. Or at the very least, let them know you are anxious to read it but will put it away until you can give it your undivided attention. They'll appreciate knowing that you find it important.

4. Learn to laugh. One of the most important things in all of life is to not take yourself too seriously. If you don't want any hassles with your parents, then learn to take it easy on yourself. What's happening to you might feel like the end of the world, or you might be feeling things you've never felt before—whatever it is that they are discounting, you have to practice laughing it off. This can help you in all areas of life, because from now on there will always be someone, somewhere, who won't validate your feelings. They'll think you've gone off the deep end or you're too emotional. Believe me, I know that of which I speak. Most of my life people have thought I'm a little out there emotionally. I'm passionate, and it can freak people out. But I had to learn to just get over worrying about what *they* think. I don't need others to validate how I feel . . . okay, maybe I do, but I've learned to find a few close friends who will sympathize with me and tell me I'm not crazy. As for the rest, I just expect them not to get me. So don't get all freaked out when your parents aren't getting you. Even though this might sound impossible, it is a goal worthy of your time and energy.

As a parent you can teach your child to learn to laugh things off and not take others' comments so personally by modeling the concept yourself. Don't take troubles at work so personally and don't whine about messes you've gotten into or problems that can really be laughed off and moved past. Your kids are watching how you react to the world around you, so help them to stop the stress and worry and learn to laugh at themselves a little more.

What to Do When They Just Don't Get You

If you don't feel like your parents understand, if they tell you that you don't or, worse yet, *can't* feel what you are feeling, don't fight it. Shut up. Tell them you understand their feelings, and then talk to someone who does understand. Some good alone time with God can be just the remedy for the misunderstood. Good music, pen and paper, and the good ol' Book will change your life in more ways than you can imagine. Think of this stupid time in your life as a call to drop everything and get close to God. When you truly have no one else who will listen and understand, God becomes the most real. So take advantage of the pain and use it to get next to God. Praying for your parents or even for yourself in dealing with them can really change your life. Believe me, it works.

4 Things Not to Do When Your Teen Is Having an Emotional Crisis

Don't roll your eyes.

Don't call them "overly dramatic."

Don't tell them, "It's not that big a deal."

Don't allow them to speak rudely or abusively to you. (Being emotional doesn't give them permission to disrespect anyone!)

Ideas to Consider

I love books. They are one of the best ways to add to your wisdom and the wisdom of your child. Here are a few titles I recommend for emotional meltdowns and turmoil. These books really help people focus on the truth and not concentrate so much on the junk in their lives. A positive outlook can work wonders for your child. Check out these books and give them a read to see if they are a good fit for your child.

As a Man Thinketh by James Allen

Telling Yourself the Truth by William Backus

The Lies We Tell Ourselves by Chris Thurman

The Christian's Secret of a Happy Life by Hannah Whithall-Smith

The Big Talk

Big talks can be stressful to all the parties involved. I can't tell you how many parents I've talked to who dread the big sex talk. Issues of great importance can create lots of angst for both you and your child. But as in all areas of life, your child's first exposure to a healthy understanding of expressing important topics is (or should be) in the home. That's why the more you can work at practicing an open and loving relationship at home, the more you can help your child learn how to package, express, and ultimately share their thoughts and ideas. Every parent I know wants to avoid arguments and explosive discussions at all costs. So how do you help your child to tackle the big ideas and still maintain the peace?

Wouldn't you love to be the first one your child comes to when they have pressing questions about life or emotional issues that they need help with? If that doesn't always happen, then how can you help? The happiest home, from a teenager's perspective, is one where their parents have time for them—time to listen, time to talk, and most of all time to just be with them. If you are having trouble getting through to your teenager, then maybe you can try a few of these ideas and see if you can't forge a bond that will help both of you to communicate better. This is very similar to what I told your teen in *Stupid Parents*. If you are both on the same page about this kind of stuff, I guarantee that things can get better between you. So let's go over a few of the basics.

The Trust Bank

In *Stupid Parents* I explained to your child that trust is of utmost importance when it comes to parents. If you can't trust your kids, then it's very hard not to attempt to control them, argue with them, and essentially keep the battle raging. Your teens need to understand that trust isn't something that happens overnight. If they've lost your trust over time, then rebuilding it will take time. An author friend of mind, Dr. Bill Harley, explains that in relationships, we all have "Love Bank" accounts with one another. Every day we are making deposits and withdrawals. The more deposits you make, the more withdrawals your account can withstand. The same is true with trust. **The more deposits, or positive experiences, you share with your child in the area of trust, the more freedom they can be allowed.** But the more withdrawals they make to that trust account, the less likely their balance will cover their exploits. The focus for your teen should be to build up their account with you so that they can improve your relationship, thus making it easier to communicate with you about the big issues.

The same thing can be said of the trust account you have with your child. If you have made many deposits that have built up their trust in you as someone who will listen to, love, respect, and care for them, then they will be much more eager to come to you for the big issues. But if lately you've been making a lot of withdrawals in the area of trust, you've got some deposits to make. For example, let's say your daughter comes to you to talk about having a crush on a boy at school. She wants someone to talk to and share with, but she'd be very embarrassed if other family members were to find out—especially her brother, who would never let her hear the end of it. If you betray her trust by blabbing to her siblings or whoever else she's put off-limits for this topic, then you've just taken out a huge deposit on your trust account.

Your child has to know that your word means something. Your yes must mean yes and your no mean no. Consistency in trust will help your child desire to come to you with the big stuff.

Give Them Attention

Whether you're unaware or it seems painfully obvious, the truth is that your child craves your attention. They might seem distant, too busy, and unconcerned about family involvement, and they might even say they want you out of their lives, but that isn't the case at all. Though they do crave their space and much-needed time alone and with friends, that doesn't mean they don't want anything to do with you, even though they might say they do.

Some parents make the mistake of believing everything their child says. So when they hear, "I don't want to do stuff with you, Mom. I just want to be with my friends," they react out of raw emotion, feel sorry for themselves, and then resent their child for removing themselves from the family. That's a mistake. Teenagers don't always mean exactly what they say, because they feel an inner tension between the kid and the adult inside of them. You have to be the parent and translate. Most often what they mean is, "It's time for me to grow up. While I still need you for guidance and in case I fall, I need to do things on my own and make my own decisions, and you are smothering me." It doesn't mean, "Please leave me alone forever and never get involved in my life." So don't get hurt when your child seems distant. You have to keep your eye on the truth: that teenagers still need parental involvement, just in a different way than when they were little.

In *Stupid Parents* I said something very similar to this to your teenager. I explained to them how you need their time. Funny, but it goes both ways. You need their time and attention as much as they need yours. But both of you might be having a hard time coming to that conclusion and making it happen.

The answer? Well, as usual, it rests firmly on your shoulders. Though I encourage your teen to find ways to spend time with you, you are really the person in the position of authority to make that happen. **Spending regular time in the presence of your teen doesn't go unnoticed.** Even if you are just in the house when they come home and you don't say more than "How was your day?"—they notice. When you are available to them, they take note and subconsciously add deposits to your trust account. Your presence in their life means more than they will ever be able to tell you. So do what you can to be available. That might mean cutting back on time at work, creating family times, and missing out on some of your personal distractions. I'm not chastising you for your way of life, but I want you to understand what your teenager is really thinking, although they may never tell you. *Your presence matters.*

So think about ways to make time to spend with them. Eat dinner with them. Find a show you both like and watch it together. Go to the mall. Whatever it might be, just be with them. Don't push yourself into their lives, but make opportunities that might appeal to them. If they have hobbies you know nothing about, learn something. **Just being available to them is the first step in getting them to share more of their lives with you.**

Another way to make deposits into their trust account is by being happy for them. Care about the things that are important to them, and pat them on the back for their accomplishments and victories. Even if it doesn't seem like much to be happy about, put on a smile. It will mean the world to them.

If you keep doing what you're doing, you'll keep getting what you're getting. Is that good enough for you? If the answer is no, then get creative. You might be saying, "But I've already tried to get involved in my child's life, and they don't want anything to do with me." Okay, then look at the things you've done, mark those off your list, and try something new. The truth is that your presence does more to build that trust account than anything you could ever say. If you've been too busy for your child in the past, make a change. If they're home alone a lot, find a way to be at home for the times when they want to talk. Communicating with teenagers isn't easy. You might choose to let them "take it from here," concentrating more on paying the bills and getting things done, but no child says of their childhood, "I'm so thankful for all the things my parents bought." Time, your time, is all they ever really remember.

Small Talk

Talking about important issues with your teen doesn't happen overnight. Sometimes you have to start with talking about little things. If you are a willing and available ear, then your child is much more likely to come to you with the big stuff. Here are a few things I told your teen in *Stupid Parents*.

> **1. Talk, talk, talk.** If you want to make it easier to talk to your parents, then put in the time and talk with them about stuff every day. It doesn't have to be deep stuff; just talk. Tell them about your day and ask about theirs. The more time you spend shooting the breeze, the easier it will be to talk with them when you have something big to talk about.

For the most part, the teen years are self-focused years, and although that can become exaggerated and troublesome, it does point to the need for your child to have your ear. They are busy assessing their lives and their position in the world, and they need your wisdom to help them figure out who they are becoming. That's why they often have such a need to talk. You can talk about yourself and the things in your life, but try not to monopolize the conversation or make it a counseling session for yourself. **The more you talk about your problems, the less they feel inclined to share themselves.** So a good rule of thumb is to listen to their lives and keep the conversation on them at least 75 percent of the time. When you talk about yourself, think of your child not as your best friend but as your child whom you are helping to grow into an adult. That means **save your complaints, agonies, and life dilemmas for your mate, your counselor, and your friends.** I'm not telling you to shut up and only listen; I just want you to understand that your teenager will feel more like talking to you the more you listen and the less you complain about your issues.

2. **Fill them in.** A good way to keep the conversations going the way you want is to fill your parents in. The more information you give them, the fewer questions they will have to ask, and the less you'll feel like you're being grilled. This is the best way to control how the conversation flows. So talk to them about the things you are doing, like where you are going, who is driving, what you'll do there, and when you'll be back. Keeping them in the loop makes them feel more secure and adds a lot to the trust factor as well. Then when it's time to ask them an important question, they'll be less likely to blow up and more likely to listen.

3. **Control yourself.** When you want to talk to them about something important, you have to remember to keep things under control. Don't blow up all over them if they

disagree with you. Keep your cool; it's the only way to help things go your way. Once tempers flare, all bets are off, and you lose any control of the conversation you might have had.

Some things to avoid: sarcasm, yelling, rolling your eyes, looking away, crossing your arms, huffing and puffing, growling.

Some things to do: Look 'em in the eye. Be calm. Listen. Give them a minute to process what you are telling them. Find points where you agree with them.

The Big Talk

The big talk can be about anything from relationship stuff to some must-have electronic they are working to convince you the merits of. Whatever the topic, big talks are of big importance to both you and your teenager. The issues that are important to them are usually issues that will ultimately affect how they feel and thus how they relate to you and the rest of the family. So having an important talk is something that both you and your teen need to understand. First of all let's look at the ideas I gave your teenagers about asking you to talk about important things.

> **Timing is everything.** No matter who you are talking to or what you are talking about, timing is everything. People who know how to get what they want know how to read situations to determine if the time is right to say what they want to say. It's like this: If your mom just got home, her arms are full of groceries, and she is moaning about her horrible day at work, it's probably not the best

time to ask her if you can spend the weekend at the lake with your best friend. Wait until the time is right. Make sure they aren't in the middle of something or upset about something and you'll up your chances of being heard and getting your points across. If you have something major to talk to them about, you might even want to make an appointment. Parents can be really busy, and this might be the only way to get their undivided attention, so leave them a note asking for a time or ask them when they will have a sec to talk. But make sure they know that it's about something important. They need to be prepared as much as you do. For the really big stuff this is crucial. They need to be ready and able to focus, so pick your time and don't spring anything on them when they aren't calm and slightly prepared.

Rehearsal. Sometimes when you have something really big to tell them, you have no idea how to say it. So spend some time prepping. Write out your thoughts and get them straight. Think about what objections or arguments they might have and what you want to say to counter those. Believe it or not, sometimes the best way to counter an objection is to agree with it. This happens in sales situations and politics all the time. Admit your plan has flaws and that you can't get rid of all of their fears, but remind them that you're worthy of being trusted (you are, aren't you?). Once you have your thoughts together, do a dry run. Lock yourself in the bathroom and talk to the mirror. Getting ready for a big talk isn't a silly waste of time; sometimes it's the best way to ensure a good outcome. So give it some thought before you dump something big on them.

The note. If you are a better writer than talker when it comes to your emotions, write out what you want to say and give it to them to read. Stay there while they read it, and then afterward talk it over. Sometimes that's a better way to make sure they get all you want to say before they start to give you their two cents' worth.

Take turns. After they've heard what you have to say, give them a chance to talk. Whatever you do, don't interrupt them or get mad at them. Bite your tongue and don't show your freaked-out-ness in your face, or you'll mess up any chance of having a calm conversation with them now or in the future. This is crucial for you to get: you are partially in control of how this relationship plays out. If you want to be free to talk to them about things, then control yourself when it's their turn to talk so that they will want to talk with you now and in the future. Think!

End it well. When you've heard their side of things and the conversation is over, end it well, even if you didn't get your way. One option is to say, "I can see that you're not convinced, but I don't want this to come between us. Would you promise me you'll just think about it some more?" and then say, "Thanks for listening." Even if they don't change their mind, if you can leave them feeling good about this talk with you, they'll be more likely to handle the next talk even better.

These ideas might seem simple or they might seem unreasonable depending on your relationship with your teenager. Either way they are steps that you both can take in order to improve communication between the two of you. When it comes to the important things in your child's life, a little extra effort will pay off. But beyond the list I gave your teen, here are some things to consider before *you* dive into the big talk.

Give them time. I encourage you to really take requests of your time seriously. As adults we schedule all kinds of things into our days, so take the step of making a time just for you and your teenager to talk about whatever it is they want to talk about. However, if they aren't begging for time alone with you to "talk," that doesn't mean they don't want to talk; it might just mean they don't want to make a big deal about it. This "understated" communication style is one that shouldn't be shoehorned into the more formal style of communication. If your kid finds casual conversation time easier, then what I suggest is being all ears when those moments come along. Watch for signs that something is on their hearts and give them your attention when those things come out. Don't scare the "understated" communicator off by being too overly excited that they are sharing or by making a big deal out of it. That will only scare them off. So watch your child's style and do your best to fit the big talk within the constraints of his or her personality.

Hear them out. Since what we are talking about here is a big talk, it's extra important that you give them time to express themselves. Don't jump on them at first breath. Don't rush to get to the good stuff, and don't change the subject if the subject seems just too scary. Take the time to listen, and allow them to get out whatever they are feeling. Then when it's your turn be sure not to correct them instantly or accuse them of anything. If you want them to listen and trust your response, then you have to be strategic. If the first thing out of your mouth is "Now, why would you think that? That's ridiculous!" or "No, no way, there's no way that will ever happen!" then you've just shut them off and they are going to feel like you just don't get it. You can get to that stuff; just don't come out swinging. Take your time to tell them that you understand their thoughts and feelings. Be sensitive and ask questions before you dive into something negative. Teens often feel unsafe about asking important stuff, because parents seem to already have their minds made up. That is a big turnoff to sharing. So do what you can to ease into rejection, if that is what has come. And make sure you understand their position or feelings before you correct them or say something that might otherwise freak them out.

Big talks can be great moments for bonding and learning for both you and your teenager. Don't fear those moments. And don't covet them so much that you are overly emotional or needy yourself. Give them space, give them the dignity of having their own thoughts and feelings on the subject, and most of all give them your wisdom in love and understanding and the result will be a happy teenager.

Having "The Talk"

The thought of talking about sex with your teen can fill you with nauseating anticipation and dread. And believe me, they aren't any more excited about it than you are. Even though this book is not about parenting but rather about understanding life from your teen's perspective, I want to encourage you to not shy away from talking about sex. In fact, I have two books on the subject written especially for teens. **In my book** *Sexy Girls: How Hot Is Too Hot?* **I talk about how girls' bodies affect the guys around them. Modesty is a lost art, and it's really where the idea of sex gets started.** So do what you can to not save the subject of sex for "the talk" but instead incorporate little conversations on sexuality and our bodies into your day-to-day life. Comment on clothing choices people make, scenes in movies, and items in the news. **In** *Technical Virgin: How Far Is Too Far?* **I'm honest and blunt about what's sex and what's not.** If you're shaking in your boots at the thought of confronting your daughter about her sexy wardrobe or outlining what really is "too far," please consider using one of these books as a tool to educate your daughter or get the discussion going. **If you have a son, consider a book my husband is writing for teen guys entitled** *The Man Manual.* Giving your kid a moral compass on sexuality can help them make the big decisions they will one day be faced with.

Look at it like this: if you don't talk to them about this kind of stuff, somebody will, and that somebody might not share your values. So be proactive, even if you're afraid. Your teen is too, so take some solace in that.

Create Win–Win Situations

Many times in the life of your child, they will want something and you won't want to give it to them. I'm sure they've tried whining, crying, and begging, all of which have probably just made your "no" louder. But learning how to negotiate and give people what they want in order to get what you want is a very valuable life skill. Teaching your child the give-and-take of negotiation can lead to success in their future careers. Of course, many things are and should be nonnegotiable, and you should express that to your child. A parent who is wishy-washy and easily swayed on important issues creates a spoiled and potentially at-risk teenager. But on some things, negotiations can and should happen. It's a way of both of you getting what you want out of a situation.

Of course, honesty is required for fair negotiations. Before your teen begins bargaining, they need to get real with themselves. Here are some things I talked to your teen about when it comes to getting what they want from you, starting with some questions I encouraged them to think about to make sure they are being honest before asking you for something that might lead to an argument.

Who are you when no one is looking? If you think you're a trustworthy, honest, and reliable person, does that hold up when you really look at yourself? Are you really all of those things? Or are you two different people when you are alone and when you are with someone else?

Are you really all that trustworthy? You might get totally ticked when people don't trust you. But think about it—would *you* trust *you*? What's your true track record? Do you do what you say you'll do when you say you'll do it?

Why do you lie? Sometimes you might lie to yourself out of self-protection. You think that if you don't trust your parents, then you can't be hurt by them. But the truth is, when you think the worst of people, you are more likely to get the worst from people. You tend to get what you expect when it comes to others. Besides, think about how you feel when your parents don't trust you. They feel just as bad when you think *they* can't be trusted with your feelings. Their track record might not be the best, but you can help change that when you start to get honest with yourself.

Keeping It Real?

In the rare case that you are all about "keeping it real," beware, because being honest doesn't mean being brutal. Sometimes in the name of honesty people will say things that are downright mean. If what you are saying won't benefit the other person, then don't say it. If it's going to make them mad or hurt, you should probably avoid it. If your sole goal is to be heard, to prove a point, or to be right, then you are dead wrong. Keeping it real shouldn't be about being heard or winning; it should be about caring and honesty. So don't say things in the name of honesty when all you really want is to prove a point or take a shot at someone.

Consistency, Consistency, Consistency

This one could be a no-brainer too, I guess, but I have to say it: being honest doesn't just end with yourself. You have to be honest in all areas of your life. You can't just decide to be honest with your parents and not with your friends. You have to be the same person all the time, because those not-so-honest moments will catch up with you. It comes down to a matter of character. Who you are consistently is your character. And people decide how to treat you and react to you based on your character. Think about it like this: If your parents hear you lying to your friends on the phone by telling one friend you're busy with homework but then going out with another friend, they might start to question your character. They think, *If she's lying to her friends, then she must be lying to us.*

Consistency also means you don't keep parts of your life shrouded in lies and other parts open to honesty. If you're an honest person, you're honest in all areas of your life. That means you're honest at home, in school, and in relationships with friends.

The Value of Memories

Building memories is a big part of building up that trust bank and building that bond between you and your child so that communication gets easier. Memories can hold a lot of cachet in familial relationships. Just think back to the fond ones you have of growing up. They stick with us for life. When you make memories with your teenager, you are putting lots of trust in your trust account. And memories don't have to be anything spectacular. Teenagers feel such an inherent need to connect with their parents (even when they don't show it) that even the little things mean a lot deep down. Things that are a tradition or done often are especially effective at creating confidence and stability in your kid's life.

So do things with them: Clean the car with your child and have a water fight. Bake cookies with your daughter. Go on vacation and spend some alone time with them. Talk to them about the memories of your childhood. And take pictures—they help everyone remember the good times. The more you can bond with your teenager, the more they will trust you and understand you, and the better your life will be. I know getting them to do things with you might seem like pulling teeth, so don't expect big commitments all at once. Find something they might like to do and invite them along. Teens can be moody, busy, or just plain bored and not give you the time of day, but don't give up. The teens I talk to say they really do want their parents' undivided attention, even if it's just while having fun.

Teaching Trust

In *Stupid Parents* I gave your child the scenario of a big talk about extending their curfew. Most kids want more time to do things with their friends, and though many of them need early curfews, some of them are trustworthy enough to deserve some more time. If your child isn't getting the concept of trust, then look over some of the ways that I told them they could help you learn to trust them more. Trust is always a key element in parent-child communication. Without trust big talks are not likely to go well, if they happen at all. So encourage your teen in these areas—not as a parent wanting control but as a lesson in negotiating with people in authority (i.e., having big talks) and getting what you want out of life by giving something of yourself and your time. Here's what I told teens about building the trust that pays off for the big talk of a curfew change:

1. **Stay in touch.** If you can stay in touch and keep them informed as to what you are doing, they will learn to trust you more. I know it seems like they are overprotective and will never leave you alone, but the ironic truth is that the more you try to help them protect you, the more they will loosen up. So here's a few ways to stay in touch:
   - Before you leave, let them know where you are going, who you'll be with, and what you'll be doing.
   - When you are out, give them a call before you come home. Let them know, "I'm just checking in. Wanted you to know I'll be leaving for home in half an hour. See you later." This lets them know that you are responsible and understand how careful you need to be when you're out at night. Remember, you have to agree with them about their fears and concerns. Life *is* more dangerous for people who aren't aware of the things that could go wrong.
   - Leave your cell phone on so they can contact you.

2. **Don't break the curfew you have.** If you want to be able to stay out later, don't miss your curfew. Sounds backward, but if you don't keep the one you have, then they won't trust you to handle a later one. If you have a good track record of being trustworthy, then they are more likely to extend your curfew over time.

3. **Talk it out.** When you've done all these things for a good amount of time, you can start to talk to them

about an extension. The amount of time you have to wait to do this varies depending on how trustworthy you've been up to now and how full your trust account is. Remember, if you want something, you have to work toward it. You have to prove yourself worthy in order to get what you want. Your parents don't owe you a better curfew. You have to earn it. It's just like life: you earn your grades, you earn your money, and you earn their trust. The sooner you realize that your actions greatly affect how you are treated, the sooner you can start to gain more control over your life. Parents aren't stupid, contrary to what this book title says. They know when you are ready for responsibility and when you aren't. So start to prove yourself today, and before you know it, you'll be getting more and more independence.

As I've said before, I'm not a parenting expert but a teen expert, so I'm not going to tell you how to set a curfew or other important family rules, but I will tell you that an informed teen is a happy teen. If they know where you stand and what the ground rules are, they are much more likely to keep them. Of course, that doesn't ensure complete compliance, but I know that if teens understand what's in it for them in a situation, they are smart enough to cooperate. If you want to help them learn to manage their lives and relationships, then work with them on areas that can bear compromising when they've proven themselves trustworthy.

The Art of Negotiation

Any good salesperson knows that overcoming objections is a crucial aspect of doing business. In *Stupid Parents* I taught your

child how to do their best to overcome your objections to the things they feel they need or want. At first this might feel like manipulation or salesmanship, but if you'll help them perfect the skill, it's really a healthy way of managing conflict. What I've asked them to do is to look at your objections, analyze them, and figure out how to overcome them. That means finding answers to your concerns so that you can be more open to the possibilities they see. Here is an example that I shared with them.

Let's say your parents won't let you get a cell phone. First of all, figure out their fears and make a list. . . . Now you have to figure out how to overcome these objections. Do this by deciding what you can do to make them understand that the things they fear won't come to pass. In the case of a cell phone, that goes something like this:

The bill. "I know you are worried about the cell bill, and I completely understand, so why don't we just get me some prepaid minutes. That way I won't be able to go over." Voila! Now they don't have to worry about big bills. Before you talk to them, decide what amount you think is best for you so you can talk it over.

Doing something dangerous or illicit. Let them know that you understand that cell phones can be dangerous if you text strangers, give your number out to people you meet online, and that kind of thing. Tell them that you know how worried that makes them, but let them know that they can track your calls on the bill each month. And if they think you're too young and are totally freaked, they can get you the Firefly phone that can only call three pre-programmed numbers. Heck, they can even manage your incoming calls.

When you think that your parents' thoughts are stupid, they get defensive and are even less likely to give you what you want. So the key is to sympathize with their concerns. See things from their point of view and tell them that you get it and that you want to help get rid of their concerns by doing this, that, or the other. You have to become a problem solver so your parents can start to see that you can handle things and be trusted. So put some time and effort into it, and you might just see a change in their attitude.

Talking too much. This one's hard to argue because it's more than likely true. The best way to fight this argument is to agree to prepaid minutes. You could also tell them, "Yeah, I know I talk on the phone too much, but this way you can have the home phone to yourself. I'll never be hogging it anymore because I'll have my own phone, and you won't have to take any messages for me anymore either."

Playing with it in class. Tell them that you understand that concern and that your teacher has a strict policy on that and you don't want to get it confiscated, so you promise to leave it in your locker or leave it turned off during class.

It will spoil you. This is one you have to prove to them by not being a spoiled brat. If other stuff spoils you, then they have good reason to believe this will too. One argument is to let them know that it's a safety thing. If your car ever breaks down or you need to reach them, you can call because you'll have a cell phone. It's not a luxury, it's a safety thing!

When you are open to your teenager's attempt to meet you halfway, you encourage independence, confidence, and a sense of trust. So don't be too quick to argue with them. Hear them out and then judge for yourself. Ultimately they have to learn to live with your decision, but hearing them out is a great way to better your relationship. When teenagers feel a give-and-take in your relationship, they are much less likely to erupt in anger or disrespect. This is just part of helping them to reach adulthood. Each time you give them more and more freedom based on their ability to handle it, you are bringing them closer to healthy adulthood.

IDeas to ConsiDer

Prepping for big talks—A lot of teens shut off their parents because they just don't think they get it. The silence of an isolated teen can be deafening. Teens who feel like they can't talk to their parents are not happy teens. If your child is reading or has read *Stupid Parents*, then they should be starting to understand the value of talking with you more freely. What they need now is for you to respond in kind. You should be able to start asking more questions and getting more involved without getting those "stupid" stares. In *Stupid Parents* I teach them the value of communication and that if they want things to be different, then they'll need to start to act differently.

Ask your teen how they feel about communication at home. Ask them if they'd like to go out to eat, and then use that as a time to talk more. Ask their opinions on decisions you are making that might affect them or even a big decision at work that doesn't affect them but shows a dilemma where either outcome has its risks. By doing this you can show them both sides of a dilemma that they're not necessarily involved in and at the same time help them understand your logic in the decision you'll ultimately make. Get them involved in the family business, even if your family business is just keeping the house in order. The more you can talk about the small stuff, the easier the big stuff will be.

Broken Trust

PART 4

Your teen has lost your trust. You can't trust her to do anything she says she'll do because in the past she's only lied and abused privileges. Sound familiar? If your teen is reading *Stupid Parents*, you might start to see a change in them. Remember, sometimes you can say all you want till you're blue in the face and your teen won't listen, but for some reason when they hear it from someone else, like me, they suddenly get it. So don't be offended or hurt that they never got it when you said it; just be glad that they are getting it now. But as I told them, gaining back trust takes time. They can't expect you to change your opinion of them on a dime. Here are some things I told them they would need to consider before things got any better between you.

Fessing Up

The first thing you have to do is admit you've done something wrong. You can't ignore that fact. You have to come clean. That's the first step in getting things back to the way they were. If you don't admit it and call your mistake a mistake, then your parents will think you haven't learned anything. Agreeing with them that what you did was wrong and being truly sorry goes a long way toward helping them to think there is hope for you and you *can* learn and grow and change and be trusted once again. Accepting responsibility is the first step in recovering your parents' trust.

If your teen has made a full confession, thank them. Teaching them to come clean is of great benefit for their future lives. But confessing can be hard, so don't make it any harder by continuing to scold them or rehashing what they did wrong. When teens feel like if they confess, you'll just chastise them unceasingly or unfairly, they are less likely to confess. So do your best to give them a thoughtful and loving response when they agree that

what they did was wrong. Understand that here I am talking about something they did that you already knew about, not some new event that you are just hearing about. What I want them to do in this exercise is to agree with you that what they did—and already lost your trust over—was wrong. I want them to agree with you that they messed up rather than argue with you that they were right.

Giving Them Time

The second thing on your plate is living with the consequences. What you did probably had results. The car you wrecked has to be paid for. The class you skipped has to be retaken, and the people you hurt, namely, your parents, have to be healed. See, when you broke their trust, you did something to their heart. You caused them to erect a barrier around it. They do this to protect themselves from being hurt again or abused again by your actions. Because that's how they feel: abused, as if what you did was done directly to them. It's a normal parental feeling. And that's why they lose their trust in you—because they've been burned. Because of that you have to give them time to heal, to get over it. And I mean *time*, because that is what it will take. They can't just forget about it overnight. So don't be in a hurry to fix things. Over time things will seem less and less huge to them, and your relationship will get better. Just remember that you can't rush it and you can't rush them by whining to them about getting over it and moving on. Give them the time they need.

Time is needed for both of you. You need it in order to be able to trust them, and they need it in order to learn discipline. It's a win-win. But whatever you do, don't hold a grudge. You're the parent, not the child. Your first job is to teach them responsibility, not to make them learn to please you and make you happy. If you hold on to their wrongdoing for an inordinate amount of time, you will give them an unhealthy understanding of forgiveness, and possibly the inability to forgive, and in a way you'll have ceded control and power over to your teen. Holding a grudge makes their actions a continual thorn in your flesh and therefore gives them control over your mind and emotions, control that they shouldn't have. **Teens need to see healthy forgiveness modeled** so that they can offer it to others as well as accept it. For how can they learn to give it if they have never received it themselves?

Changing Things

The final step in rebuilding trust is to make sure that what you did never happens again. Because if it does, then any trust you have rebuilt will go out the window, and gaining it back will be twice as hard as before. Your job is to do what you've got to do to make a difference in your life. If you keep missing class because you can't get up in the morning, then find a way to change that. Go to bed earlier. Move your alarm across the room. Ask your mom to come in and open the curtains. Whatever it takes, don't keep making the same mistakes over and over again and expect your parents to trust you. They'd really be stupid if they did.

Encourage your teen in healthy trust building. It can be hard on both of you, but trust is an important commodity for life. Sometimes restoring trust after it's been broken can seem like jumping off a cliff without a parachute. But eventually you're going to have to give it a try (the trust building, not the cliff jumping). Offering trust gives your teenager hope and a chance to learn real responsibility. Don't be too quick to offer trust—it should be a valuable moral quality that isn't taken lightly. But also don't refuse to ever trust again. Teenagers tend to rise or fall to the level of trust and hope you have in them.

Ideas to Consider

Teaching trust—Talk to your child about trust when you see the opportunity. Who do they trust and why? When did someone ruin that trust, and how soon did they give it back to them? Discuss their friends, teachers, and relatives, anyone they trust or don't trust, and make it a well-understood concept.

Learning to trust—Some teens find it hard to trust their parents. Talk to your teen about your own trustworthiness, and don't get mad if you don't like what you hear. No one is perfect, not even one, so don't be surprised if your own trust account needs some deposits. Consistency, consistency, consistency. Talk to your teen about your failures and promise them that you'll make a change.

Really Stupid Parents

PART 5

So far the stupid-parent problems we've been talking about are run-of-the-mill stupid—things that aren't really stupid but are just misunderstood by your teenager. I must confess that the things I'm going to talk about in this chapter are, well, stupid. Before you get mad at me for calling you stupid, realize that thankfully, this chapter doesn't apply to everyone, so just hear me out.

Some of the things that you did to your life before you were a parent didn't impact anybody but you. But when you became a parent, life changed. Now the things you do greatly impact your child. Your reasons for doing what you've done are yours, and I'm not here to argue them. What I am here to do is to tell you that as far as your teen goes, if you've done or are doing any of the things outlined in this chapter, you have made or are making their life more difficult than it should be. So whether you are divorced or dealing with some kind of addiction, you need to read on and figure out ways you can help ease the trauma your life has brought on your teen.

The Hurt of Divorce

When I was eleven, my parents got divorced. I didn't think much of it at first. Since I was an only child, I guess I was too busy trying to take care of each of them to think about what it meant to me. The drama in their lives was agonizing. They needed someone to be calm and in control, and that was me. I remember at that point consciously deciding that I now had to be the leader of the family. I had to take care of things because my dad was no longer going to be there. So I bucked up and became "the man of the house," at least in my mind. And my childhood ended.

Their divorce had nothing to do with me. I mean, it was all about their inability to get along. But that didn't mean I wasn't changed forever by it. Divorce is awful, plain and simple. It's never easy to deal with. It never leaves you untouched. At first I dealt with the trauma by hating my dad. He was the one who messed up; it was his fault, I reasoned, so I hated him. I was so protective of my mom that I couldn't see that it takes two to tango. I had no idea until I got a lot, lot older that this wasn't my battle to fight or take sides in. My job was to live my life and live it with both parents, even if that meant doing a lot of traveling. But instead I cut myself off from my dad and spent years without him. That did a lot of damage to my mind and my heart. Not until much later was I able to finally forgive him, let go of my anger, and reconnect with him. Now we get along great. I just wish I hadn't missed all those years of having a dad. What could I have done differently? How could I have had a better relationship with both parents who did a really stupid thing? When I got much older and wiser, I finally figured a few things out.

Don't Blame the Kids

When a divorce happens, kids feel like they are the reason for it, whether it's true or not. There is no way around it. When one parent leaves, they leave more than just the other parent—they leave the kids. And kids always have the thought, even if it's only in the back of their head, that they are the reason that parent left. What your child has to come to grips with is that it is in no way about them.

Even if your life went downhill as soon as you had kids, the reason you divorced was because you and your spouse were no longer able to live with one another. You can't ever, ever, ever blame divorce on the presence of the kids. When you do, you destroy a part of them. I encourage you not to allow your child to blame themselves. The most important thing for them to understand is that the divorce is in no way about them. It's about a man and a woman breaking up. It's your relationship with your spouse that has gone south.

It will, however, take more than talk in order for your teen to believe you on this fact. Time and attention are the only things that will help keep them from being permanently scarred. I hate to tell you (because I assume that if you're reading this, you've already divorced and the damage is done), but no child is unscarred by divorce. All you can do, once the damage is done, is hope to put some salve on it and encourage a healthy response to the situation in both your child and your ex's life. And over time the scars will heal.

Humans Make Mistakes

The biggest thing that helped me get over my parents' divorce and get back to loving them both was realizing that they are only human. I used to think my dad was like Superman or John Wayne. He was my idol. I followed him around wherever he went. In my eyes he could do no wrong. So when he left, I felt like he was leaving me, although I didn't realize it right away. I knew it wasn't my fault, but I thought that if he loved me, no matter what happened with him and my mom, he would never leave *me*. But he left, so I must not have been special enough to make him stay, right? Wrong. That lie tormented my life for many years. If only I had been old enough to understand that it wasn't about me, things could have been so much better. I could have had a life with my dad. But instead I chose to hate, and I hurt both him and me.

If your child is suffering from your divorce, make every effort to be honest with them. **Don't blame your mate;** admit that it takes two to tango and talk to them out of experiences that they might understand. Dating and breaking up is often part of a teen's past. Perhaps talk to them about a break up they had and why they couldn't make the relationship work. If my parents had been more honest and helped me as a teenager to understand that each parent is only human, it would have helped me immensely. It turns out it was someone other than my mom who pointed out to me that my dad was human and made mistakes just like all of us. It sounds silly, but this simple insight really helped me get perspective. And offer forgiveness.

Don't Make Your Ex a Villain

No matter what you feel about your ex, you can't share that with your child. When you insult, criticize, or indict your ex, you hurt your teen. Remember, your child is half your ex, and as you attack their other parent, they feel the pain of that attack as if it were a personal attack on them. The best gift you can give your child is the gift of two loving parents. Even if you are divorced, you can both respect one another in front of the kids and allow them to have parents they can respect. When you work at destroying the image of the other parent in your child's eyes, you take away from them the gift of a functional, healthy relationship with that parent. And as a result, you create a dysfunctional kid.

Think about it like this: **the more you explain the shortcomings of your spouse, the more your child will attempt to heal those shortcomings through assorted relationships with other people.** In a strange human reaction to divorce, girls whose fathers are absent and cheating often choose men just like their fathers. It's their attempt to vicariously heal the relationship with their father through another man. The best thing you can do for the mental health of your child is to speak highly of your ex, their parent. Any teen you talk to will tell you that it hurts down in the core when they learn how horrible, sinful, or mean their parent really is. So no matter what the truth is, I encourage you to hold back the gory details of your relationship from your child.

Don't Let Your Kid Get a Divorce

I encourage both you and your teen to make a conscious effort not to allow the parting parent to disappear. When your teen decides to divorce the ex from their life, the separation can haunt them the rest of their lives. If your ex isn't violent or abusive to you or your teen, then your child will benefit most from continuing a "normal" relationship with them. Many teens decide to side with one parent or the other, and that is a very unhealthy choice. When they do that, more times than not they end up resenting the parent they've disowned. At first they think it's the smart choice, but over time resentment, anger, and depression creep in. The teens who handle divorce the best are teens who stay involved in both parents' lives.

Forgiveness

When we don't forgive someone, we allow the pain they inflicted on us to remain a gaping wound exposed to the elements. Unforgiveness only makes things worse. **Your teen might think the best way to get back at one or both of you is by refusing to forgive. But when they forgive, they heal.** Forgiveness seals up their wound and makes them almost whole again.

How can you help your child to forgive? First it's important to understand the definition of forgiveness. According to Webster's dictionary, to **forgive means "to give up resentment of or claim to requital for" or "to cease to feel resentment against."** Forgiveness doesn't mean they have to tell you that it was a good idea that you split up. It doesn't even mean they have to say, "It's okay you got divorced," because the truth is that it *isn't* okay you got divorced. Divorce is rarely okay for the family. **What forgiveness does mean is that they are going to stop resenting you for it.** They are going to get over it. Because if they don't get over it, then they'll be haunted by it until they do.

~~~~~~~~~~~~~~~~~~~~~~~~~~~~~~~~~~

Stay Close

It's important for your teen to maintain a consistent relationship with each of you, even after the divorce. If one of you moves away, that distance is very destructive to your child. It might seem impossible to stay in the same place, but if your child's health is important to you, do all you can to keep the family in the same city. If your spouse moves, move closer so your child can maintain a relationship. Sound drastic, too hard, or unbearable? I'm sorry, but I'm just trying to help you understand the mind of your teenager and the way your life affects theirs. When one spouse moves to another city, the pain of divorce strikes again, even deeper. It's like a divorce happening all over again. If you notice your child is depressed or angry and one of their parents is now out of easy reach, you might want to consider bringing the family back to the same town.

Don't Make Them Pick Sides

I'm sure that your spouse did some nasty things. They hurt you, broke your trust, and damaged the family—but remember, it takes two to tango. **When you encourage your child to pick sides, you make the pain of divorce even greater for them, because they love you both the same and making them choose makes them feel like they are dishonoring your ex.** So in order to keep the drama to a minimum, you can never ask them to pick sides. That means not asking them to get involved in your battle. Don't run things past them, explain how awful your ex is, or put them in the middle of anything. Don't use them to fight your battles. And that means no giving them notes or messages to pass to your ex.

Allowing them to pick sides might seem like being real with your teen or extra honest, but it is nothing of the sort. I know how a single parent and a child can bond through these times, almost like best friends. But you're not. I know a newly single parent can be lonely, but your child needs you as a parent more than you need a confidante. Do your best to keep your fight to yourself and allow your child to have two wonderful parents.

You might feel like you're being a hypocrite or lying to your child when you pretend your ex is a good person, but that's not the truth. Hypocrisy is saying or believing something is wrong but doing it anyway. And I'm here to tell you that leaving out the bad parts about your ex and only sharing the good with your child isn't wrong. It's actually the best way to produce a healthy, happy teenager. For example, if your ex left you for another person, that's horrible—but you don't have to tell your child that they wanted that other person more than you. Even if the ex said, "I want this person more than my family," don't tell your child that. It will only hurt them. When you tell your child anything negative about your ex that isn't necessary for them to know, you are only thinking of yourself. It might make you feel good to slander your ex to your child. "After all, he is an awful person, and my child needs to know that," you reason. You want *you* to be the good one, not your spouse. But that's all about you, not about your child. If what you are telling your child won't make their life better, happier, or more complete, then when it comes to divorce, they probably don't need to hear it.

You aren't telling a lie if you make your ex look good in front of your child. The truth is that your ex *is* a good person for your child—they are that child's parent. To you, they are not a good person, not a trustworthy person. But like it or not, they are the parent of your child, and that will never, ever change. So your choice is to either leave your child the legacy of two good parents or slander your ex and leave your child with as much dislike for them as you feel. That isn't fair. Make sure not to make your divorce your child's divorce. Give them the gift of feeling they have two good parents.

Life Isn't over

In *Stupid Parents* I tried to show your child that there is life after divorce. They need to hear it from you too. Here is what I told your child about refocusing their life and working through the hurt.

You might feel like a monster truck has run up on your life and pinned it to the wall, but that doesn't have to be the case. Your life can go on—in fact, it must. Keeping focused on your goals, your hopes, and your dreams can help keep your mind clear. Spend some time writing out your dreams. Think about what you want to do, where you want to go, and who you want to be. This divorce will be not the death of you but the birth of you, if you let it. Use the negative for good. Trials and tribulations, if accepted as something good, can only make you stronger. The most successful people in the world aren't people who have had blessed lives but people who have lived through turmoil and destruction and come out on the other side. So focus on your future, not the past, and let this stupid mess become a step toward the next big thing in your life.

Talk It Out

The biggest and best way to work out anything in your life is on your knees. Spend time talking out your pain and anger with God. Whether you pray by your bed or spend time journaling, the more you do this, the more you'll be free from the stupid choices made for you by your parents.

You can also talk to someone like a counselor or pastor. Sometimes just telling another person how you feel can make you feel a whole heck of a lot better. Just make sure that you aren't using this as an excuse to wallow in your pain. Getting over things sometimes means giving it up to God, trusting him that he'll work this junk out for you, and then getting on with your life.

Divorce is never a happy thing. And it should never happen in your life, but it does happen. Trust me when I say you can live through it and make it to the other side. You can have a good relationship with both parents, in most cases, and you can learn to trust again. Don't let their stupid mistake become your future. Choose to forgive them and get over it so you don't end up repeating it yourself when you grow up.

*Source: National Association for Children of Alcoholics, www.nacoa.org

The Harm of Drugs and Alcohol

In most households the parents are trying to keep their kids from using, but in some it's the other way around. If you are a parent who is under the influence of drugs or alcohol, your child is suffering. They are experiencing a sense of helplessness and neglect. They are at the mercy of your ever-changing moods. It's something no child should have to live with.

I'm not a drug and alcohol specialist. And I'm not telling you anything you don't know. But understand that you gave up your right to party, play around, and experiment when you had a child. Now, until they are at least eighteen, your job is to love and care for them more than yourself. I know you want more for your child than you've had, but you have to understand that if you are addicted to drugs or alcohol, your child is four times more likely to become addicted as well.* It's time to get help for the sake of your child and their future. Visit your local church for a referral to a local recovery group or treatment program *today.*

1 in 4 kids under 18 lives in a family where a person abuses alcohol or suffers from alcoholism.

National Association for Children of Alcoholics,

www.nacoa.org

The Danger of Being Overworked

Drug abuse and divorce are obviously stupid parental blunders. But there is another kind of parental stupidity that is more subtle. These parents aren't abusive or mean. They aren't drunk or fighting. They just aren't there. In fact, their kids rarely see them. The kids let themselves in the house after school. They make their own meals, do their own thing, while their parents make guest appearances at the beginning and end of the day. Many a family functions this way, and many a parent misses the incredible wound they are inflicting on their child. When parents spend more time away from home than at home, the kids notice. Sure, they appreciate all the good things your hard work provides—the plasma screen, the big house, the great cars, the in-ground pool, and all the clothes they could ever want. But ask any teen and they will tell you that they would trade all of that for more time with their parents.

As your child gets older, it's true, they require less and less of your time. You might have had one parent at home with them most of their lives, but now they are doing things on their own and don't seem to need you as much. And though that's true on the surface, underneath it all they still need your presence. I talk to many teens who complain that their mom and dad seem to think getting things and working are more important than their kids. They bemoan the fact that all they ever get from their parents is things, and they wish in their heart of hearts that they could just get some *time*. **The biggest lie ever told was that kids are just as happy with quality as quantity.** From what I've heard from their mouths, that isn't true. **Teens need quantity in times of "peace" and quality during times of crisis** or when they hit milestones like appearing in the school play or getting their heart broken for the first time. Just knowing you are in the house and

available while they do their own thing in their room or with their friends means the world to them. Having you available to listen to them, share with them, and be with them is of tremendous importance to most teens.

If you are having problems with your teenager, consider the fact that most kids get into trouble between 3:00 and 6:00 p.m. Why do you suppose that is? The obvious answer is that they have no adult supervision. But that's not all. The truth is, even if there is adult supervision in the form of a substitute caregiver, they are potentially still struggling with issues of neglect or abandonment that can lead them to act out in anger and even violence. I know the words *neglect* and *abandonment* are *really* strong, but these are the words and feelings of the teens and pre-teens I talk to. Of course there are financial concerns and cost-of-living choices to be made, and they are never easy. But in the mind of your child, you have to be aware of the way they think. Leaving your children to their own defenses or in the hands of a part-time, non-parental caregiver, damages the hearts and minds of children by making them believe that something else (i.e., work) is more important to you than they are.

Research confirms that children are less likely to get into trouble when a responsible adult is watching them. "Children aged 12 to 18 are not just more likely to engage in risky behaviors, but they are also more likely to benefit from positive mentoring. In a study published by the American Academy of Pediatrics, researchers found that eighth-graders who are unsupervised more than 10 hours a week are about 10% more likely to try marijuana, and twice as likely to smoke cigarettes or drink alcohol as are eighth-graders who are never without adult supervision."

Denise Mann, "Who's Watching Our Teenagers?" MedicineNet.com, October 29, 2001, http://www.medicinenet.com/script/main/art.asp?articlekey=51701.

If you are having trouble communicating with your teenager, ask yourself some hard questions: Could she possibly misconstrue my use of time with neglect? Am I too busy to slow down and hang out with him? Am I stressed when I get home and run ragged from my hectic schedule? Do a lot of fights erupt because I just don't have the time or the patience to put up with them any longer? If any of these ring true, then you might need to consider some changes in your lifestyle. Consider that no one ever looked back on their life and fondly recalled how many things their parents owned. People don't look back longingly at "the great Range Rover I grew up with" or wax sentimental about the maid who came in each week to pick up after them. No, what we remember most are those amazing talks we had in the kitchen till 2:00 in the morning. Or the smell of pancakes on the griddle each morning. Your teenagers covet and dream of the times you spend with them, not on making money for them.

I'm not suggesting you spend every waking moment with your child or follow them around every minute they are at home. All I am saying is what teens are telling me, and that is that they wish they had more time with their parents, even at the expense of things. I know not everyone can downsize anymore and survive, but many of us *can* downsize. Trade that car payment in for a cheap car with no payments. Move out of that house that eats up half of your take-home pay and into a more manageable one. That might seem like a lot of work just for someone who's only going to be living there a couple more years before moving out, but isn't that the point? If you are having trouble connecting with your child and you want a change, this might be what is needed. Just consider what you may be modeling for them as their "life coach." What is more important, your child or your possessions? A lifestyle change is an investment in the life of your child—while you still have the opportunity.

Still don't believe that teens prefer quantity over quality? Then consider this: Would your child prefer to have three pieces of the finest French chocolate or a bag of Tootsie Rolls? If given the choice, would they prefer two medallions of beef with shoestring potatoes and glazed carrots at a fancy and expensive restaurant or a large pizza? When it comes to perishables like food and your time, teens time and time again choose quantity over quality.

Teen Talk

I'm going to share with you what I told your teen to do if you have a problem with working too much. If your teen approaches you like this, please listen and don't take offense. They aren't in your life for much longer, and soon you can get back to taking care of you, living your dreams, and doing whatever you want. You'll be alone in just another few years, but until then consider the fact that your home will be more peaceful and happy if at least one of the parents is more available and less harried. Here is what I told teens in *Stupid Parents*:

> So talk to them. Help them to understand what you need from a parent and what you don't need. This isn't a time to cut them down but to love on them. Tell them how much you like being with them and how much you miss them. Let them know that you have enough things and that you would much rather never get another new outfit than continue to miss them every day. Whatever you feel, let them know

about it. They might just be thinking that you love *things* as much as they do so you want them to keep working all the time. So have an open discussion with them. They may or may not see the light and make some major changes in their life, but either way, at least you've done what you can.

The next thing you can do is make an effort to get into their schedule. If they can't quite swallow the "please work less so I can spend time with you" plea, then you might have to try something more intrusive. Get on their calendar, but make sure it isn't for an event centered around spending money. This is where the truth comes out. Do you really want *them* more than *things*? If you do, then come up with some free stuff you can do together. The more you take money from them, the more you show them that they have to continue to work hard to support you. So it's time to think about your life and what is important to you. Things or people. Love or money. Try writing out your thoughts. Tell your parents how you really feel about them and about the things they provide. Do your best to live a life without being materialistic, and see if you can't help them to come to the light side.

Ideas to Consider

Many parents just don't understand why their kids are acting up and getting into trouble, and oftentimes the answer lies with the parent's availability. I understand that many of you can't make drastic changes, but if you are having troubles with your teen, please consider some preventative measures—stopgap changes, if you will.

- Keep them busy. Help your child get involved in constructive after-school activities like sports and other adult-supervised recreation.
- Know where they are at all times. A cell phone can help you keep tabs on them, but don't use it as a babysitter.
- Randomly check that they are where they say they are.
- Know what your kids are doing online and watching on TV.
- Talk, talk, talk. Become as much a part of their lives as you can to help keep the lines of communication open.
- Let your neighbors know when the kids are alone so they can keep an eye on their activities.
- Forget the nonessentials. Spend as much time as you can with them, even if it means not cleaning the house today or leaving the dishes for later. Just find time to invest in what counts—your teen's life!

Living with a Single Parent

When my parents first got divorced, life didn't seem too different. But after a few years, things started to pop up in my life that made me feel the sting of separation. I lived with my mom, and my dad lived about an hour and a half away. Many times I felt like I needed him and the things a dad takes care of, but I didn't get access to him, and because of that I resented him. Fortunately, we've worked through those issues, and now he feels more like a dad again.

But back to my story: Living with just my mom was a good experience. We are great friends now, and I think it has a lot to do with us doing life on our own. But as I look back I can see a few things that weren't the best option for a kid growing up. I don't resent her for it; she didn't know any better. She was just doing the best she could. We both have grown over time and have come to understand more about the importance of the family and the roles inside the family. But way back then we just didn't know the best way to do things, so we did what came naturally. We became best friends.

A lot of parents feel like their child is their only ally in the battle with their ex. Not only that, but they are so upset from losing their mate that they have a real concern about losing the child as well. In order to ensure that never happens, many parents decide to avoid making their teens upset or mad at them. At all costs they want their kid to like them more than they like the ex. "After all," they reason, "I've had one loss in my life and become an enemy to one family member. I can't bear to do that again." And the best friend parent is born.

Still, other parents aren't so concerned with the child leaving as they are with causing as much pain as they can to their ex. And so becoming best friends with their child seems like a good way to hurt their ex even more by proving who really is the best parent. They might even have a hint of hope that when the offending parent sees how wonderful life is with the rest of their family, they will come crawling back, longing for the days when everything was wonderful. It's human nature to want to protect oneself by harming an offender, but that doesn't make it right or even healthy.

Some parents end up in the best friend parent role simply out of a need to have a partner. Their spouse is gone, and loneliness sets in. They need a friend, and a teenager is so "almost adult" in their thinking and attitudes that they feel like a true friend. These parents want to do things with their child that friends would do. They are more lenient than most parents and spend a lot of time getting personal with their child, sharing their own feelings and shortcomings with them as if they were a best friend.

That's how it was for me and my mom. She and I were (and still are) best friends. I didn't have to do anything around the house that a normal kid did. I didn't have chores. I didn't have to cook, or do dishes, or even clean up my room if I didn't want to. We talked about everything together. She knew all the things going on in my life, and I knew all the things in hers. And it seemed great. I have a lot of very good memories of growing up. But that doesn't mean we were healthy.

Looking back, I can remember feeling the void of not having a parental figure. If you would have asked me if I felt safe, I would have had to say, "Not really," and I can tell you exactly the reason why. After the divorce my mom started dating this man. He was an okay guy, I guess, though it is rather creepy thinking of your mom dating—but I digress. The problem came when one summer they broke up. He hurt her pretty bad, and she was a wreck. I can remember her crying for days. She was so sad. I felt so awful for her. And I became her shoulder to cry on, like any best friend would. I listened to all the pain flowing from a jilted lover.

I can remember that at that point I made a decision. I was about thirteen years old, and I said to myself, "Well, it's time for me to step up and take charge. The one who should be parenting isn't in any state for that, so I'll have to do it." I remember being so concerned for my mother that I started thinking of all the things I should do to take care of her. Essentially I looked at all the things my dad had done around the house and decided I would start doing them. I remember thinking something really silly but life-changing. I said to myself, "Well, I can start changing the lightbulbs and fixing the toilet when it breaks." Why I thought of those two things first, I have no idea. But it seemed like a good place to start—to start to become the parent, that is.

And therein lies the problem with becoming best friends with your child after a divorce: **teens can't truly bear the responsibility for the emotional life of their parents.** They aren't wired for it. They are the children, the ones who need to know they have stability at home to rely on. They are the ones who are going through emotional upheaval and need somewhere safe to land. When the parent shows their emotional upheaval and relies on the child to be a sounding board for it, they leave the child alone and wondering who will take care of them. And as a result, the child skips their childhood and goes straight to adulthood without completing the necessary steps to get there. In other words, they grow up too fast. For a teenager, being the grown-up in the family is a very uncomfortable feeling. It leaves them feeling fearful and unsure of their future. It can breed a sense of dread, loneliness, martyrdom, and anger in teens.

Being best friends with my mom was not the worst thing in the world for me—in fact, I love having her as my best friend now, and

I think a close relationship with your parents is wonderful. I just know that being a kid is wonderful too. So if you are a divorced parent, I encourage you and your spouse to both do the adult thing and agree not to dump your emotions onto your child. Talking about your marital disasters with your child is not healthy and does not breed contentment or security in your child. Divorced parents must find other adults with whom to share their burdens emotionally and even practically. Find a divorce support group at an area church. Find people who will listen and offer healthy advice for living through the agony of divorce. Just don't bring your kids into it.

If you notice that your child is starting to take on more and more adult responsibilities, make sure that it is in keeping with their age and not a hurried attempt by them to fill the gap left by the parting parent. Sure, chores will need to be done, but it is best to avoid assigning them anything that would seem to burden them with all the things the parting parent used to do.

When you talk to your teenagers about the divorce and your new lives, be sure to explain to them that this doesn't mean they will need to take care of you now or that you are going to rely on them more now. That's a statement a lot of parents make: "I'll have to rely on you more now that Dad is gone." Oh, what that does to their little hearts! Even if it is true, don't make that statement. To a teenager that sounds like a re-placing statement—"You are now the dad for both of us." So talk to them and explain that you are still the parent and things aren't going to be that much different when it comes to their role in the family. When parents do their best to remain the parents and keep things as normal as possible, they help their teens deal with their own grief without adding to the burden.

Family Feud

After my parents divorced, not only my mom but also her entire family hated my dad. I can remember listening to my grandmother and aunt tell me how awful he was and how he didn't do this and he didn't do that. It was a hate party every time they were around, as if they thought I would take all that information back to him and tell him off for them so that he would hurt even more. What they didn't get is that the only person they hurt was me. They gave me a skewed image of my dad that wasn't true. He was only human, he made mistakes, but I didn't deserve to be emotionally dadless because of their hatred for him. I took what they said and internalized it, and I decided I hated him too. So for five years I didn't talk to him. I even changed my name. I didn't want anything to do with such an awful man. How sorry I am that I did that! I love my dad. He was once my hero, and he is again, only in human form this time. I just wish I hadn't lost those five years thinking I had to feel as awful about him as the rest of my family did.

Parents Who Are Looking for Love

After a divorce, most parents eventually begin to date again, and when they do, it can be a horrible feeling for the kids involved. Most of us can't imagine our parents with another person, and the thought of there being new kids on the horizon can be devastating. I remember when my dad remarried not long after he divorced my mom—I was crushed. The only photo I have of his wedding is one of me standing silently in front of him weeping. I felt the loss of my family even more vividly now that he had a replacement wife. But the thought of other kids coming from that marriage paralyzed me. The entire prospect of my dad with another woman was devastating to me. And many teens feel the same way. But even if they don't—or don't act like it—parents still need to take some precautions when diving back into the dating pool.

It's crucial that you don't think of your child as your best friend when it comes to dating. We all want to talk about the excitement of a new love and all the amazing things they do, but that can be a terrible thing for your child to have to hear. You might have such a desire to share your happiness and think, *What can it hurt for them to know how happy I am?* Let me just tell you, from your teen's perspective, it's awful, even though you're happy. The only way to put it is to say that it's just creepy for them to think about you with a person other than their other parent. Teens know

60% of second marriages
end in divorce.*

3/4 of divorced men and 2/3 of divorced women remarry.*

* Robert E. Emery, *Marriage, Divorce, and Children's Adjustment* (Thousand Oaks, CA: Sage Publications, 1999).

the ins and outs of dating better than anyone, so they know what you're doing when you're on your dates. Think about how sick it feels to hear your parents talk about their sex life. Now imagine how awful it is for your kids to imagine your dating/sex life with a stranger. It's not a good feeling.

Some teens might not mind the conversations at all; in fact, they might welcome them. They've seen you sad for so long that they are glad you are finally happy. They understand your need for a partner, and they secretly long for a new complete family. The danger here for the mind and heart of this teen is that if and when you break up with this person, your teen has to go through the same emotional pain you are going through. After all, they've sunk just as much hope into this one as you have. You've broken up with not only your boyfriend but their future father.

For the sanity of your child, I encourage you not to share your dating life with your teen. Some parents even go so far as to make the date a pseudo-family member. They bring them to family functions, invite them to many dinners, and practically move them in (some actually do move them in). This "playing house" is unhealthy not only when teens do it but also when their parents do it. **Bringing a non-permanent person into your teen's life and pretending they are permanent is like playing Russian roulette with their hearts and lives.** Teens run the risk of falling in love with the new parental figure and losing them when you can't make it work. Worse yet, many children are abused by the very person their parent is falling in love with. For the safety and sanity of your teenager, I encourage you to keep your dating life to yourself until you are ready to make another commitment. And I pray that this time, for the sanity of your child, you won't allow this commitment to be broken.

Dating shouldn't be off-limits for divorced parents, but consider the notion that putting it off until your kids are out of the house or

at least insulating your kids from the new crush until it's an exclusive relationship with some track record would be kinder to your children. **Getting your kids involved in potential heartache is just too much of a risk.** Consider spending your free time with your child in order to keep busy and help them to recover from the loss of a much-loved or at least much-needed parent.

Child abuse is 33 times higher when the mother is cohabitating with a boyfriend who is not the father of her children, than in an intact family.

Patrick F. Fagan, "The Child Abuse Crisis: The Disintegration of Marriage, Family and the American Community," Heritage Foundation Backgrounder No. 1115, June 3, 1997, at http://www.heritage.org/library/categories/family/bg1115.html.

Partner violence was twice as high among romantically linked but unmarried couples as among married couples.

"Marriage Boosts Parents' Mental Health" Statesman.com, September 28, 2006 (HealthDay News), http://www.statesman.com/health/content/shared-auto/healthnews/prnt/535193.html.

Stepparents and Your Teen

As I've already mentioned, when I was about fourteen, my dad married my *first* stepmother. She was only about ten years older than I was, had no kids, and didn't want any, especially me. For the next thirteen years she made my life miserable. I cried on the day he married her, and I smiled on the day she left him. Now I have another stepmom who is a million times better. She is actually the one who helped me restore my relationship with my dad. She works hard to keep us communicating, and she does all she can to make me part of their new family. So when it comes to stepparents, I've lived through both the bad and the good.

When I was younger I didn't really know what to do with a mean stepmom. It was such a new thing for me that I had no idea how to deal with the potential jealousy and resentment, and there weren't any books like *Stupid Parents* around to help me. And so I ran. I ran from my first stepmom *and* from my dad. And that was one of the biggest mistakes I could have made and my mom could have allowed. Resenting my dad and moving as far as possible away from him emotionally was destructive not only to our relationship but to the myriad of relationships I had while in high school and college. If you have or are looking for a new spouse, consider some important points in order to keep your teen as healthy and happy as possible.

In 1992, 15 percent of all children were living with biological mother and stepfather and 1 percent were living with biological father and stepmother.

Robert E. Emery, *Marriage, Divorce, and Children's Adjustment* (Thousand Oaks, CA: Sage Publications, 1999).

Child abuse is six times higher in the stepfamily than in the intact family.

Patrick F. Fagan, "The Child Abuse Crisis: The Disintegration of Marriage, Family and the American Community," Heritage Foundation Backgrounder No. 1115, June 3, 1997, at http://www. heritage.org/library/categories/family/bg1115.html.

You're Not the Boss of Me!

Just because you picked them out, had a wonderful wedding, and plan to live happily ever after doesn't mean your child had any real say in the matter of choosing your new mate. And chances are, they had *no* say. You fell in love and that was that, and now they've got a new parent. Now comes the real test of the relationship: handling the children. Who's the boss? Who makes the rules? Who enforces them? But more importantly, how does your teenager handle your new decisions? I'm not going to tell you how to design your family, but I am going to tell you what I told your teenager about living in this new environment. Perhaps it will give you some insight into ways they can learn to coexist with a new authority figure.

So what about when she tells you what to do? What about when you don't like her rules or her way of doing things? Can you revolt? Call for a mutiny, or better yet a new stepmom? Boy, I wish I could have way back when he married wife #2. But you can't do any of those things. Suddenly there's a new sheriff in town, and you had no part in the election. So what do you do when they tell you what to do? Do you say, "You're not my mom!" and run out of the room? Do you complain to your dad about how evil she is? Or do you give up all that your mother taught you and start to live as your step-monster, I mean stepmother, has decided you will live?

Well, my answer goes something like this: Remember that thing I said about living under authority? And how you can't overthrow your parents or quit them? Well, same goes for steps. They aren't (and might never feel like) your parent, but while you live in what is now their house, you have to live under their secondary authority. Of course, your biological parent is your real authority, but they have decided that this new person is the kind of person that they can trust not only with their heart but with you as well. So the deal is, if you want peace in the home, then you can't buck and kick every time your step asks you to do something. You have to decide that learning to live under authority is the best option for your mental health. You don't have to like the way they do things; all you have to do is remember that the best way to make this relationship work is to go with the flow. No two homes are the same, so I guarantee you that this step won't run things the way your other parent runs them. Things will seem awkward, not normal, and I totally understand. Heck, to me, my stepparents' households have never felt like home, but I never had to live with them full-time. I always got to go back to normalsville with my mom. But if you have to live with your step full-time, then take heart, because things will eventually settle in. It will begin to be home to you. Not the home you were used to but a new home. Just remember, if you want a fight you can always get a fight, but do you really want your home to be a war zone?

Everything you've read in this book till now applies to the stepparent, because it's their home you are living in now. Even though they aren't the boss of you, they are the boss of the household. So practice what you've read and know that ultimately it isn't about how things get better or whether they ever get you or not, but it's about you and your character. What you learn and put into practice in this home will help shape your life. You can't be in charge of who your parents marry, but you can be in charge of how you react to them. And your reaction has a huge effect on what they do and say to you. The payoff from respecting your step, even if deep down you resent them, is huge. A resented step is not the best person to live with, but when you set them free from your anger, you can start toward a happier home life.

So here's the deal: you have to forgive them. I know that they might be the reason your parents broke up. They might be totally awful and horrible to live with. They might want all of your parent's attention. But whatever the trauma, you have to forgive them. If you don't, then you'll resent them, and resentment makes for a nasty home life. It's like something rotten under your bed just stinking up the place—it only gets worse and worse with time. So you've got to do some spring-cleaning. Decide to get over the offense they committed in exchange for happiness. I mean, you can hang on to your anger, but you're the only one you're hurting. Sure, you might make things uncomfortable for your step, but you're living in your own personal hell until you can get over whatever it was they did or are doing to you or the ones you love.

Who knows? Maybe if I would have made a bigger effort to get to know and care for my first stepmom, she would have been nicer to me. She might have seen that I was not her enemy but her ally. She might have grown to be a good friend. But no use crying over spilled opportunity. I believe that we tend to get out of people what we expect to get out of them. If you think highly of people, they are more likely to treat you kindly than if you think poorly of them. Our thoughts really do have a lot to do with how people interact with us.

> A particular train of thought persisted in, be it good or bad, **cannot fail to produce results.** A man cannot directly choose his circumstances, but he can choose his thoughts, and so indirectly, yet surely, shape his circumstances.

—James Allen, As a Man Thinketh

The Competition for Attention

Many times stepparents feel jealous of their spouse's kids. They feel like the love of their life loves someone else, the kids, more than them. And that's probably true, but it's not the end of the world. I wish my first stepmom would have understood that I could never have replaced her. She was my dad's wife and I was his daughter—two decidedly different roles. Her jealousy of me only made both our lives miserable.

I think stepmoms the world over struggle with jealousy. It's got to be hard for them to see someone else get the kind of love from their man that they want to get. That's one of the dangers of marrying someone with kids—you never truly get them all to yourself. Stepfathers' problems tend to stem more from their competitive nature. They aren't as prone to jealousy, but they are still very competitive and might feel a need to compete for the mom's attention. Either way, stepparents can add an interesting dynamic to the family they've joined.

But sometimes the jealousy is on the other foot, and the child feels jealous of the new parent and the time they spend with you. In *Stupid Parents* I encourage your child to remember that no matter how much you love this new person, they can never replace your flesh-and-blood children. And truth be told, there ought to be enough love to go around. It isn't always the stepparent's fault that kids feel replaced; sometimes the parents themselves overcompensate for having kids by taking some of the time they used to have for their kids and giving it to their spouse. Either way, jealousy is not a good thing for your child to be living in. And the best way for them to learn to live with the feelings they have is to better understand where everyone is coming from. When they understand the things I've been talking about here, they can start to get less emotional and consider the reality of the situation. Take a look at how I tried to help them understand.

When you can understand where another person is coming from, you can deal with them a whole lot better. If you can come to terms with the fact that things are different now and your parent's time is going to be split between you and this new person, then you can start to allow them that time to be together. And hopefully the step will start to allow you time with your parent as well. It might not seem like it right now, but there is always hope. Things don't often stay the same. And if you are willing to give love and consideration when you aren't getting any in return, you are one step closer to changing things. Someone has to be the bigger person here and make the move to improve things, and it just might have to be you.

Love is an amazing tool in the hands of someone who knows how to use it. When people feel loved and respected, they tend to soften up. So don't be so quick to hate, but look for opportunities to care for others. It's no surprise that the two greatest commandments both include love. It truly is what makes changes in the world we live in. So find ways today that you can love without getting anything in return.

The payoff will one day come and the change will happen. But even if it doesn't, I guarantee you that loving on this side of heaven will only make heaven that much better for you! So stay focused on what's best; don't break under the pressure of hatred and resentment. Let love win the fight, and things will change before your eyes.

" 'You shall love the Lord your God with all your heart, and with all your soul, and with all your mind.' This is the great and foremost commandment. The second is like it, 'You shall love your neighbor as yourself.' On these two commandments depend the whole Law and the Prophets."

—Jesus in Matthew chapter 22, verses 37–40 NASB

No one can drive us crazy
unless we give them the keys.

—Doug Horton

Well, our time together is over. I hope you've found something you and your teenager can take from all this. I believe you only want what's best for your child and that's why you've taken the time to read this far. Spend time going over the ideas in this book with your teenager, and if they haven't read *Stupid Parents* already, get them involved by giving them the book. Better communication and understanding of one another can make life so much easier.

You have a big job growing up a teenager into an adult, but you are perfectly suited for it. You are in a position to share the wisdom you've gained throughout your life and allowing your teenager to learn by experiencing victories and making mistakes of their own.

I encourage you not to allow your child to usurp your authority but to understand your role as a parent and theirs as a child. As you teach them to live under healthy authority, you are giving them a successful future. The more your teen can learn to control their thoughts and actions on a particular subject, the better they can survive and thrive in this world.

I hope you have enjoyed the journey. Again, I'm no parenting expert; I have simply tried to share with you what your teens are thinking and going through in their day-to-day life with you. And I hope that a better understanding of that will help to bring peace back to your family.

Let me leave you with this one last thought: The older you get, the easier it gets to deal with your children. Their time living with you is almost over. You are in the homestretch. Don't let a minute go by when you aren't loving the fact that they are still with you. Enjoy all you can, and learn to say, "This too shall pass"—because before you know it, they will be gone.

www.notsostupidparents.com

Hayley DiMarco writes cutting-edge and bestselling books including *Mean Girls: Facing Your Beauty Turned Beast*, *Marriable: Taking the Desperate Out of Dating*, *Dateable: Are You? Are They?*, *The Dateable Rules*, and *The Dirt on Breaking Up*. Her goal is to give practical answers for life's problems and encourage girls to form stronger spiritual lives. From traveling the world with a French theater troupe to working for a little shoe company called Nike, Hayley has seen a lot of life and decided to make a difference in her world. Hayley is Chief Creative Officer and founder of Hungry Planet, an independent publishing imprint and communications company that feeds the world's appetite for truth. Hungry Planet helps organizations understand and reach the multitasking mind-set, while Hungry Planet books tackle life's everyday issues with a distinctly modern spiritual voice.

To keep the conversation going log on to
www.notsostupidparents.com.

And for more on Hayley's other books check out
www.hungryplanet.net.

"Feeding the World's Appetite for Truth"

What makes Hungry Planet books different?

Every Hungry Planet book attacks the senses of the reader with a postmodern mind-set (both visually and mentally) in a way unlike most books in the marketplace. Attention to every detail from physical appearance (book size, titling, cover, and interior design) to message (content and author's voice) helps Hungry Planet books connect with the more "visual" reader in ways that ordinary books can't.

With writing and packaging content for the young adult and "hip adult" markets, Hungry Planet books combine cutting-edge design with felt-need topics, all the while injecting a much-needed spiritual voice.

Why are publishers so eager to work with Hungry Planet?

Because of the innovative success and profitable track record of HP projects from the bestselling *Dateable* and *Mean Girls* to the Gold Medallion-nominated *The Dirt on Sex* (part of HP's The Dirt series). Publishers also take notice of HP founder Hayley DiMarco's past success in creating big ideas like the "Biblezine" concept while she was brand manager for Thomas Nelson Publishers' teen book division.

How does Hungry Planet come up with such big ideas?

Hayley and HP general manager/husband Michael DiMarco tend to create their best ideas at mealtime, which in the DiMarco household is around five times a day. Once the big idea and scope of the topic are established, the couple decides either to write the content themselves or find an up-and-coming author with a passion for the topic. HP then partners with a publisher to create the book.

How do I find out more about Hungry Planet?

Use the Web, silly—www.hungryplanet.net